Options Trading Guide For Total Beginners

Zainx M. Hardin

Introduction

This is a financial guide that explores options trading as a strategy to create monthly or bi-monthly income. This book starts by demystifying options and explaining their potential benefits, such as risk reduction and wealth acceleration.

The book emphasizes the importance of setting up a strong financial foundation, becoming financially intelligent, acquiring assets, and increasing savings for investments. It advocates building systematized businesses, investing in market leaders, and using options to increase the speed of money in your portfolio.

Readers are encouraged to focus on essential aspects that great investors consider and to create a watchlist of "heavy hitters" in the stock market. Assessing profitability is another crucial skill covered in the book, providing insights into effective covered call strategies and how to enter and exit positions. The text also discusses the timing of selling stock and buying-to-close call positions and provides guidance on rolling positions from one month to the next.

Structuring your stock investment portfolio is the final focus of this book, helping readers understand how to create a balanced and effective portfolio for their options trading strategy.

In summary, this book offers a comprehensive guide to options trading as a strategy for generating monthly income. It covers a range of essential topics, from understanding options to developing a structured investment portfolio, making it a valuable resource for those interested in exploring options trading.

Contents

WHAT THE HECK ARE OPTIONS, ANYWAY?

O ptions are a financial derivative used in the stock market to either buy or sell shares in a company at an agreed upon price and date. Options come in two different flavors - a call and a put - that can be either bought or sold. All option trading strategies are based on only these four factors. This guide focuses on just selling calls.

The conservative call option strategy of selling covered calls offers you the opportunity to create some additional monthly income in addition to the gains made with any stock value appreciation. This strategy works well when the markets are slowing trending upward (what is known as a bullish trend) or when the markets are flat month to month.

Of all the option strategies available to the stock investor, selling covered calls is the simplest to implement. The basic idea is to "rent out" your shares of stock on a monthly or bi-monthly basis. Just like in an apartment rental, you're paid a premium up front (the rent) in doing so. To "rent out" your shares, you must own at least 100 shares of stock for every option contract that you sell.

When you sell your contract, the buyer on the other end of the transaction now has the right to buy your stock at a specified fixed price, known as the strike price. The buyer can do so only when the stock price is at or above the strike price.

They have up to a specific date known as the expiration date to do so. The buyer can then choose to buy your stock at any time before this expiration date once it is at or above the strike price. Sounding good so far?

You may be saying to yourself, hold your horses Scott. That sounds like a losing proposition. Why would anyone want to rent out their stock only to see it being sold a few weeks later? Don't you need to stay invested in the stock market to create wealth? Isn't that bass ackwards, I mean ass backwards?

No worries, my little padawan. Even if your stock is called away, that is sold at or prior to expiration, at your agreed upon strike price, you can still profit from the situation. You're about to learn how to properly structure each covered call position so that you can optimize your profitability.

If you had set your strike price above your initial price paid for the stock, you not only get to keep the premium from selling the call option, but you have also captured the capital gain of the stock rising from its initial price to the strike price. As well, you're positioned to take advantage of the next opportunity that presents itself.

For example, I've found myself being exercised, that is to say having my stock called away, on a couple of occasions. Good news? It didn't cause any fatigue, nor did it leave me breathless. When that scenario unfolded, I was able to pick up both the call option premium and the capital gain on the stock price having appreciated in value. Not a bad scenario, wouldn't you say?

Just rinse and repeat when the opportunity unfolds. Imagine benefiting from a similar scenario.

When you learn how to control your cash flow that is being generated from your options, you'll see the full potential behind selling covered calls. You may have this burning question in the back of your mind.

Why Use Covered Calls?

Selling covered calls has some great benefits. Here are the top three reasons why you should consider implementing them into your overall stock investment strategy.

Benefit #1: You tap into monthly or bi-monthly income.

You can generate a nice stream of additional income from selling option contracts on stock that you already own. Selling options has been known to generate double-digit returns for one's stock portfolio over the course of a year. Like beer this is proof that God loves us and wants us to be happy.

Conservative covered call strategies can produce a consistent stream of income that will surpass market averages without increasing market risks.

Benefit #2: Options reduce your exposure to risk.

When you're paid a premium for selling an option contract, that cash reduces your initial cost price or basis for the stock. In other words, your breakeven point, should the stock decline in price, has been lowered by the amount of the premium deposited directly into your brokerage account. Yes! You do get paid up front when you sell option contracts. Isn't that cool?

You've essentially built in a margin of safety for preserving your initial capital. Over time as you continue to write covered calls, which is another way of saying selling covered calls, your cost basis of the stock will drop to zero.

When this happens, you're generating a cash flow from an initial investment whereby you've recovered all of your initial capital even with a stock that may not have appreciated in stock price. You'll be in the enviable position of playing with the house's money, as they say in Vegas. Can you imagine how reassuring this scenario would be?

Benefit #3: Options accelerate your wealth creation.

Generating cash flow from multiple sources, such as options and dividends, accelerates the velocity of your money in moving your capital into better and better investments.

Also, being able to generate income from multiple sources allows you to have access to capital for future opportunities when they present themselves.

And don't forget the compounding effect of re-investing your premiums. Re-investing your proceeds gets you that much closer to reaching your point of critical mass with your investment portfolio. More on that in a moment.

As a novice options trader, there's no reason to start out learning complex strategies. Some of the simplest most conservative strategies can be the most lucrative. I haven't been this happy since I graduated from diapers to the poddy. Yippy skippy!

What about Stock Market Volatility?

Ya! What about stock market volatility, Scott? The traditional approach to investing in the stock market is to place your hard-earned dollars in the hands of a mutual fund advisor. The buy, hold and pray my stock goes up approach touted by most mutual fund advisors has an inherent flaw.

By parking your money and leaving it in the hands of your advisor, you run the risk of losing a substantial part of your built-up equity by trying to weather out any storms in the stock market. Now, granted a long-term buy and hold approach to investing can generate descent returns over a 30 to 40-year period of time. Don't get me wrong.

The problem is not with seeing a return over time, it's how much of a return you'll be receiving down the road. Actively managed mutual funds can charge portfolio management fees that erode your wealth accumulation.

For example, if your mutual fund generates an average return of 9% and your management expense ratio (MER) is 3%, you haven't lost a growth potential of just 3% due to fees, you've actually lost a 33% growth potential (3/9 or 1/3) due to fees. Ouch! That hurts. You may be better off head butting a cactus.

I recall the look on the face of a close colleague of mine who was foaming at the mouth as he expressed his frustration with his mutual fund advisor. No, he wasn't bitten by a rabid squirrel. His advisor had him switching from one fund to another over a 10-year period, chasing after returns. It was driving him nuts. His overall portfolio grew only by the additional deposits he had made over the years. He felt like a hamster turd - real shitty.

Who wouldn't be frustrated and ticked off with a system that's supposed to build wealth over time? What's even more aggravating is that markets do not climb upwards in a straight line. The very nature of the stock market is that it is subject to wild swings, not unlike the waves of the ocean during a storm.

A little stock investment knowledge allows the informed active investor great wealth creation opportunities despite what the markets are doing.

Watching your investment portfolio losing <u>book value</u> (that is what its currently worth on paper) by normal market volatility and not knowing how you can capitalize on great investment opportunities as they unfold is both disheartening and discouraging. You may feel completely at a loss and totally helpless in not knowing what to do.

By knowing more about how the markets function you're able to incorporate money-making strategies that capitalize on the normal fluctuations of the stock market. This is what you'll learn how to do by the end of this book - cross my hear and hope to die.

Is options trading too complicated and risky for the average investor?

True, getting started in options can initially be challenging. The specialized language unique to options trading can scare off some investors. As in learning any new skill, the initial learning curve can also be steep.

However, once you've picked up a few basic skills and have been able to apply that newfound wisdom, you'll find that your ability to make money whether the stock market is going up, down or sideways is well worth the effort.

Once you master the special language and start using the three conservative money-making option strategies described in this guide, you'll wonder why more investors aren't doing the same thing.

Covered calls allow you to "hedge" your investments so that you're able to better control your risk level.

The term <u>hedging</u> refers to the use of either a call or put option to reduce the risk of capital loss. Hedging can provide some insurance or protection for your stock holdings. This is exactly what covered calls provide.

Not only does selling covered calls provide you with an opportunity to generate additional cash flow, it also cushions your stock from the effects of a temporary drop in the stock price. In effect, options can be used to reduce your overall portfolio risk and make you some additional cash at the same time. Sweet deal, wouldn't you say?

During high periods of market volatility, the amount of income available from options sales can easily exceed 20% annually. Who wouldn't want to learn how to generate returns of 20% just from their options plays? Most people would give their right kidney for returns like that, am I right?

Unfortunately, I can't make you any promises as to what sort of returns you'll generate. Promises are like babies. They're fun to make, but harder to deliver.

The major advantages of combining individual stock picks with options is that you're able to take advantage of the compounding effects of option premiums and stock appreciation, as well as being able to mitigate your downside risk through the use of strategically placed positions.

The challenge you currently face is in increasing your financial intelligence to a level where you can profit from a combination of simple yet effective strategies that'll generate massive cash flow. Let's explore how to do just that.

~

SETTING YOURSELF UP FOR SUCCESS

L et's set the stage in this chapter for what follows. Before we delve into the actual process of finding market leaders that you can invest in, it may be beneficial to quickly frame your success moving forward in the big scheme of investing. Starting with a fundamental question …

How Do Self-Made Millionaires Build Wealth?

Most wealth builders focus their time building three types of investments, namely:

1. Improving their financial education in areas that'll have a positive impact on their ability to grow their capital under various market conditions.
2. Acquiring cash flowing assets, whether it be in the stock market, real estate or commodities.
3. Building systematized businesses that are able to generate passive income while they sleep.

Here's an overview of these three smart investment vehicles and how they might help you down the road.

(1) Becoming Financially Intelligent.

Congratulations! The act of picking up this guide is yet another step you've taken to building your wealth. Having taken the time today to explore ways of improving your current financial situation says a lot about who you are.

You've stepped from the realm of a wanna-be wealth dreamer to actually doing something about your financial situation. Now it's time to start creating a better life for you and your loved ones. It's happening now with you developing the most important tool that you can hone - your financial intelligence.

When you improve the quality of the financial information that you use in your decision-making, you set yourself up to be in a better position to tap into your financial genius. Pretty important concept, wouldn't you say?

(2) Acquiring Assets.

All wealth builders acquire assets that put money into their pockets. They invest in those asset classes with a proven track record of generating cash flow from the investment.

The top three general asset classes that most people are familiar with as investment opportunities are:

- equities (stocks),
- real estate and
- commodities.

As you know, this guide focuses exclusively on the world of stock investing and shows you step-by-step how to implement an investment system that systematically puts money into your pocket every month.

Real estate is the second general asset class that active investors like to invest in. You'll often see real estate investors buy an investment property and then rent it out as a means of generating a monthly income. Sound vaguely familiar?

The covered call strategy of "renting out" your stock in the options market, whereby you receive a monthly cash premium for doing so, is similar to having a rental real estate investment.

Investing in commodities such as oil wells, precious metal mines or alternative energy ventures is the third asset class that can provide a monthly check in the form of royalty payments.

Each of these three asset classes has specific benefits, risks and rewards. In general, the most cost-effective and time-efficient way to generate cash flow is through the stock market.

Unfortunately, rental real estate or specific commodity plays tend to be a little more capital intensive to start off with. However, as your wealth begins to accumulate, you may wish to further explore investing in these asset classes.

Whether you choose equities, real estate or commodities as your preferred asset class, please keep in mind that your focus should be on putting money into your pocket through positive cash flow. That would be slicker than a muskrat slide after a rain storm, wouldn't you agree?

(3) Building Systematized Businesses.

To give you a complete perspective of the three primary areas where the resources of effective wealth builders can be allocated for creating sustainable wealth, I'll briefly mention building sustainable businesses.

Building a low-start-up cost, systematized business that runs on its own even when you're not present is appealing.

It's definitely one effective way to exit the 9 to 5 rat race and be the master of your own destiny. No longer do you need to succumb to your employer's chosen path for you. And the best part about working for most employers is coming back home at the end of the day. Am I right?

Be aware that starting any business requires hard work and patience. Don't confuse "get rich quick", which is a distinct possibly for you, with "get rich easy".

Of course, when you have realistic expectations and develop an appropriate business attitude that factors in the amount of time and effort required to build your second or third stream of income, this becomes a viable option. And just because you may not have the money right now, doesn't mean that you shouldn't have the hope.

The Path to Profits:

In order to build sustainable wealth over time, you'll need to channel your efforts into three specific areas, namely:

(1) Increasing your savings for investments.

Having access to investment capital is the foundation of building wealth. If you do not make saving for investing a priority - you cannot invest - if you cannot invest - you cannot create the lifestyle that you dream about.

The first path to wealth creation remains your ability to move capital into investment opportunities as a result of your saving-to-invest regimen.

Whatever approach you decide to undertake in order to make this happen, start by making "investmen-titos", small consistent contributions to your stock portfolio.

(2) Investing in Market Leaders.

Buying stock of those businesses that are market leaders in their sector lends itself to a higher probability that the shares will appreciate in value more so than average stocks in that sector. Mr. Market likes businesses that have solid growth in earnings and cash flow.

The key to the whole process is to take the time to find a fundamentally solid stock with great upside potential, which is exactly what we'll explore in detail in the next chapter. That should make you happier than a clam at high tide.

(3) Selling option contracts on stock that you own.

Piggy backing off of the previous two focus areas, is the sale of options contracts on stock that you already own. In essence, you receive a cash premium in your brokerage account when you agree to sell your stock shares at a specific price on or before a pre-determined date.

You're about to discover how you can generate a monthly flow of cash into your account, by renting out your stock similar to how a property owner rents out an apartment unit. This process can generate a conservative monthly cash flow of 2 to 3 percent when properly structured, which is what you'll learn how to do by the end of this guide. Scout's honor! Moving on to ….

Two Key Wealth Building Factors:

Unfortunately, many investors give little thought as to how long they're going to hold onto a stock position. They don't have an exit plan.

This often means that they automatically adopt a "buy, hold and pray the stock will go up" approach to stock investing. They're hoping that come hell or high water they'll end up on top with sizeable gains after a few years. But what if things don't pan out?

Given this insight, a fundamental question you need to be asking yourself is:

How long am I willing to tie up my capital?

Put another way:

When do I need to move to another investment opportunity with more strength and momentum that allows me to further accelerate my wealth-building?

Let's take a moment to explore two key wealth-building factors right now starting with:

Factor #1: Increasing the Speed of Your Money.

Successful investors do not park their money and forget about it. They move their money around into better and better investment opportunities. This holds true whether you're talking about stocks, real estate or other business opportunities. This strategy is known as "increasing the speed of your money."

Every investor's goal should be to acquire cash flowing assets and to continually seek better opportunities that'll get them closer to realizing their dreams. The old buy and hold strategy that worked during the last major bull market of 2012 to 2019 is showing signs of being less promising.

We need to consider those strategies that'll work in today's markets that have experienced surges in equity and commodity volatility, not to mention the increased uncertainty. In order to accelerate your wealth building process, you have two plans of attack to consider:

(1) Increase the velocity <u>within</u> investments.

You'll want to focus your profit-making potential on the combination of dividend payments, option premiums and stock appreciation in your core holdings. Each component adds to your overall return compounding over time to quickly reach a point of critical mass.

(2) Increase the velocity <u>between</u> investments.

By getting into the habit of monitoring potential investment opportunities, the odd one could present itself when it meets your specific buy criteria. Then by acting quickly to move your money, you can take advantage of that window of opportunity.

When you spend a small amount of time each week assessing potential investments, you increase the chances of moving into these profitable opportunities.

Yes, making money in any market requires some ongoing analysis. Doing nothing is harder. You never know when you're done. Wouldn't you concur?

And, having you work smarter than harder at building your stock portfolio is fundamental to your success. Which brings us to the second factor to building wealth.

Factor #2: Reaching a Point of Critical Mass.

In the beginning, the compounding effect of your investing slowly builds over time. After a certain period of time, the compounding effect of your cash flow that you're generating from your investments will exceed your expenses and provide you with your desired lifestyle.

When this happens, you've reached a point of critical mass with your investing. This magic number is just that. It's different for each and every one of us, depending on one's cost of living and desired lifestyle. Capiche?

Once you've reached this point of investing prowess, financial freedom is just around the corner. Do you now see how you could be in a better position to empower yourself and take concrete action?

Let me close out this chapter with some sage advice.

The Top 5 Things Great Investors Focus On:

When you look at the lives and accomplishments of some of the greatest investment minds that have come along a central question come up. What does it take to consistently earn money in the markets today? Here are 5 golden nuggets of wisdom to help get you closer to your investment goals:

Focus #1: **Have a "will try hard" attitude all the time**. Commit to learning something new about stock investing every day. This means being proactive and developing some positive daily learning habits.

For example, could you set aside some time each morning reading for 15 to 20 minutes or listening to an audio book before heading off to work or elsewhere? You bet your sweet bippy you can.

You're doing it now by exploring the wonderful world of covered call writing. Keep in mind that everything you want in life is on the other side of your fears. Some of those fears are a lack of understanding of what potential lies just ahead.

Focus #2: **Be teachable**. It's important to keep an open mind about learning new approaches and concepts. When you show a willingness to learn, you step out of your comfort zone, which allows you to change the way you think about yourself, others and hopefully the world of investing.

Being teachable means that it may require that you let go of a belief you've held close to your chest like a religious artifact. Be coachable and be okay with not knowing.

Focus #3: **ASK, listen and learn**. The acronym A.S.K. – Always Seeking Knowledge should guide you in your personal growth and development. Keep fostering your curiosity and move you to another level of understanding about investing. Do so by tapping into the wealth of knowledge of those experts who have gone before you.

Actively go out and seek answers to your most pressing questions either on blogs, video posts or in the print media. What got you to this point in your life won't take you to the next level.

Focus #4: Be creative in how you squeeze learning time into your daily routine. Can you combine your exercise time with reading or listening to a personal development tape? How about listening to an audio program while walking the dog or on your morning commute? I bet you're currently doing this right now. Am I right? What's important is to establish a daily routine of self-development that'll move you to the next level. Your income can only grow to the extent that you do.

Focus #5: Use adversity as your university. Avoid blaming yourself, others or your dog for mistakes you make with your investments. Mistakes ultimately result in an opportunity to learn. Your temporary failures are not a problem; they now become a project. Re-frame your thinking and attitude to look at each problem as just another challenge. Keep this in mind for all of your future investment opportunities.

Realize that your road to success will always be under construction.

Time to boot, scoot and boogie into the next chapter.

≈

3

CREATING A WATCHLIST OF HEAVY HITTERS

F irst things first. Before outlining where to find potential stocks to invest in, let me briefly touch on setting up an options trading account. All major brick-and-mortar brokerage houses as well as online discount brokers offer option trading platforms.

Ideally, setting up a tax-free brokerage account like a Roth IRA offers some distinct advantages over a 401(k) or traditional IRA.

In a nutshell, a Roth IRA:

- Allows most people with earned income the ability to invest.
- It gives you greater flexibility as to what investments you can hold in your account.
- It'll generate tax-free growth as opposed to tax-deferred growth.
- And it allows you to take out your original contributions any time you want, regardless of your age, without taxes or penalties.

As you know, we're all born free and then we're taxed to death. So, it makes sense to structure your investment portfolios to reduce the effects of taxation on your holdings.

Often your best bet is to set up an account with an online discount broker. Online brokers typically offer lower transaction fees.

The higher fees often associated with brick-and-mortar brokerage firms will erode your cash flow growth over time. As the martial arts master says to his young accolade: "Choose wisely, Grasshopper."

All online discount brokers will allow you to sell covered calls from your IRA. Start the set-up process by doing a little comparative research online. This should yield a couple of promising discount brokers who offer low fees and good support. Just follow their account set-up instructions for being able to sell covered calls on stock that you own. This is typically an easy process to follow as it requires no previous trading experience, nor do you need to meet strict capital requirements as with more advanced option trading scenarios.

Let's move on to taking a detailed look at how to go about identifying potential stocks that you could possibly invest in down the road.

What we're going to do is compile a list of stocks that we can check out later to see if they show some promise as an investment. This chapter is going to focus on where to look for those hidden gems. We'll be placing our prospects on a watchlist that'll guide our future in-depth research.

An Ariel View of the Markets:

Wouldn't you love to own a portfolio of stocks that has the greatest potential for consistent capital appreciation over time with limited downside risk? Me too.

The challenge is in knowing which stocks to place on your watchlist of top candidates. Here's my favorite stock selection strategy to help you with the decision-making process.

Start by looking at what the overall economy is doing. You want to narrow down those sectors or industries that offer the best growth prospects over the next couple of years. And why only look at the next year or so?

Typically, the economy expands and contracts on average every 5 to 6 years. It becomes extremely challenging for any investor to make realistic growth projections for time periods greater than 1 to 2 years.

What I like to do is take a short-term top-down macro (or bird's eye) view of the economy. Put yourself in the muddy boots of a forester who focuses on looking at the health of the overall forest before checking out the individual trees that can be harvested.

You need to focus on identifying market trends that'll support certain sectors and then select those industries that'll benefit from the trends. Once you have a feel for the overall market, you can drill down and select the best businesses in each industry or sector. Following me so far?

Here are three questions to help you get started in assessing the current market environment:

(1) Is the economy expanding or contracting?

A Google search of government websites will give you a feel for what the economy is doing. As well, several major financial websites like Yahoo Finance, MSN Money or Morningstar have blog posts, videos and links to this type of economic data and reporting. Look for official announcements indicating the state of affairs of the economy.

(2) What is the overall trend in the stock market?

Take a look at a technical chart of a broad index such as the S&P 500, which can be found online at websites like Stockcharts.com or FreeStockCharts.com. Being visual in nature, you can quickly assess whether or not recent market conditions have been neutral (a flat graph), bullish (a positive upward trending graph) or bearish (a negative downward trending graph).

(3) What is the interest rate trend?

When interest rates are rising, there may be competition from high-quality fixed-income instruments (like bonds) impacting how money flows into and out of the stock market. When interest rates climb, many institutional investors shift their capital out of the stock market and into bonds. As well, higher interest rates affect economic sectors differently.

The major stock market exchanges loosely group businesses into 11 economic sectors that represent key areas of the economy. Here are some general observations that you can use to your advantage in screening for promising economic sectors to invest in:

- The retail industry benefits from a low inflation rate trend.
- The mining sector benefits from a high inflation rate trend.
- The consumer staples sector is affected the least by a slowdown in consumer spending. Consumer staples are those products that we all tend to purchase on a recurring basis, like toilet paper and beer. Well … maybe not the beer.
- The consumer discretionary sector benefits from a strengthening economy since more individuals have discretionary income to spend.
- Both the health care and consumer staples sectors do better in a slowing economy. Investors tend to move capital into these defensive stocks in a bad economy.

- The financial sector is negatively impacted by rapidly increasing global debt.

Once you've identified those sectors that show some promise, you can then start screening for top-notch businesses that are the market leaders in their respective industries.

7 Trends to Keep Your Eye on:

Continuing with our top-down approach, here are seven global trends that could provide you with some potential stock investing opportunities.

Trend #1: Cannabis

There's no better time to get in at the ground level of the cannabis industry than right now. Cannabis stock prices are attractively priced. The North American market in 2017 was conservatively estimated to be a $10 billion industry. Fast forward to 2023 and many experts are expecting it to grow to at least $35 billion. Being a young industry, there's huge growth potential over the next decade as major players expand their footprint across the globe. As local jurisdictions clean up the illegal market, you'll see a shift in buyer behavior to safer, more regulated products offered by the big boys.

Trend #2: Senior Healthcare.

The fastest growing sector of the American population is the over fifty crowd. This segment of the population is requiring more services related to health care as it ages. Drug retailers and pharmaceutical companies should see steadily increasing demand for their products, even if a recession hits us. Of particular note, is the growth potential of the edibles market in the cannabis industry as more and more seniors explore the health benefits of CBD-rich products.

Trend #3: Artificial Intelligence

Artificial intelligence growth is fuelled by increasing demand for cloud-based applications and services, along with the need to provide technological solutions to handling big data applications. We're also seeing huge demand for AI-powered industrial robots and natural language processing. This industry is expected to grow from $20.7 billion in 2018 to $202 billion in 2026, which represents an annualized growth rate in excess of 30%. As Sponge Bob Square Pants would say: That's pretty impressive alright!

Trend #4: Alternative Energy.

As technology advances so does the feasibility of integrating more and more green energy solutions into our current power grid. The recent international movement targeting greenhouse gas emissions and the dangers of global warning, is in the mainstream media. Companies to explore are those that specialize in wind turbines, solar panels, fuel cells, geothermal heating and the harnessing of ocean currents.

Trend #5: Blockchain

Blockchain is a digital ledger that uses cryptography and timestamps to build stable and secure records. The blockchain industry got its start in the cryptocurrency industry. The technology has incredible applications in bolstering security and "proof of concept" in the health care, financial, manufacturing and retail sectors. This industry is expected to show annualized growth in excess of 35% over the next 5 years.

Trend #6: Building Materials.

China and India are two of the largest consumers of building materials in the world. Their economies will continue to grow over the next decade. Companies seeing a steady growth in sales as a result of increasing demand for construction material are those producing products such as copper, steel and wood. Also look at companies whose job is to move building materials globally either by rail or ship.

Trend #7: Counter Terrorism.

Global political instability is a growing concern. More and more developed nations are spending considerable sums of money on tracking, monitoring and detecting terrorist activity. Those companies that specialize in newly developed counter terrorism technology should benefit financially over the coming years.

Hopefully this snapshot of several megatrends will help point you in the right direction for potential investment plays. It's just a matter of googling each sector and looking at various reports within each sector then placing those major players of interest on your watchlist. Let's dive even deeper into the process by having you explore the following 10 informational sources.

10 Super Sources of Information to Help You Find Potential Stocks:

Once you have an idea as to which economic sectors might be profitable, your next step is to identify potential investment candidates. The following tips should save you some time conducting your initial research in discovering those profitable businesses that you can later assess in greater depth. Remember, your initial goal is to generate a list of potential stocks that you can analyze further once they're on your watchlist.

(1) Invest in What You Know.

Time to do some reflective thinking. What are your passions, skills and interests? In order to invest confidently in any one business, it definitely helps for that particular business or industry to have some personal meaning to you. When you have a strong personal connection to the industry in terms of first-hand knowledge and experience, the greater your chances of selecting a wonderful stock that you're willing to follow up on.

Ask yourself:

- What hobbies do you pursue that might give you a greater insight into a particular business or industry?
- Which businesses do you spend your money at?
- What talents do you have that give you insights into certain business models?
- What passions do you have that have given you a certain level of expertise?

Now, brainstorm a list of those potential industries and specific companies that you would enjoy researching based on your answers.

(2) Check Out Free Websites.

There are numerous finance websites that can help narrow down your prospects. Free stock screening tools can be found on several free websites such as Yahoo Finance and MSN Money. Using the search capabilities of each site you can zero in on potential industries that might be of interest and then drill down to come up with a list of businesses that should have meaning to you.

(3) National Business News Channels.

Business news channels like CNBC, PBS or your favorite national business news station can offer insights into upcoming market leaders in certain sectors and industries. Sometimes you can get great leads on businesses to consider in your initial investigation by watching TV programs like WealthTrack on PBS, Jim Cramer's Mad

Money (Boo-yah!) or Fast Money on CNBC. Jot down the names of those potential companies that tweak your interest. These are options to consider, right?

(4) The Print Media.

Books, magazines and newspapers are another source of potential companies to explore. Before buying any book or magazine or thinking about subscribing to any newspaper, see if you can save yourself some money by checking out the various sources at your local library. There are a multitude of magazines to choose from, such as Forbes, Fortune, Smart Money and Smart Investor. As far as newspapers, check out the Wall Street Journal or The New York Times for ideas.

(5) Stock Investment Websites.

Worth investigating is to see what words of wisdom you can gleam from various stock investment blogs and websites. There's a lot of free information available on the web. It's just a matter of doing a little bit of investigating.

You can also check out paid subscription sites such as the American Association of Independent Investors, Motley Fool's Stock Advisor, The Street.com or Investor's Business Daily for suggestions and recommendations.

(6) Watch Local TV Newscasts.

Have you noticed how the local morning news is where they start by saying "good morning" and proceed to tell you why it isn't? Sorry, I digress.

This tip piggy backs off tip #3. Many TV stations look for opportunities to showcase local businesses that are breaking onto the international scene with new technological advances or state of the art products and services that appeal to a global market. Look for those news reports that highlight growing national franchises with a local home base. You may be able to tap into that hometown advantage by getting a different perspective about a company through the local news.

(7) Explore the Business Section of Your Local Newspaper.

Businesses that are being profiled because they are able to benefit from recent government contracts, positive developments from within their industry or a growing global demand for their products or services are good candidates. While perusing the paper, keep an eye out for those national businesses that are consistently advertising not only their products or services but also their reach and influence into the international arena.

(8) Pay Attention to New Store Openings.

While heading around town, pay special attention to any signs announcing new store or factory openings. Are any major malls currently expanding to accommodate growing national franchises? A regional powerhouse may have enough momentum to take the business to a nationally recognized brand. These types of businesses could be placed on your potential investment watchlist.

(9) Check out Billboard Advertising.

During your commute to and from work, make a mental note as to which major corporations are advertising frequently on billboards. Which businesses have been consistently promoting their brand awareness? You may be able to identify companies that are aggressively marketing their goods and services and may be poised to expand globally.

(10) Observe Mall Shopping Behavior.

This is one of my favorite strategies for finding great stocks. I've been known to walk aimlessly through the local mall analyzing consumer behavior. What I'm looking for are those stores that seem to always be busy no matter what time of the day.

There you have it. Hopefully, these 10 tips will provide you with some insights into which businesses to investigate further.

I like to place them on a watchlist that I create on an electronic spreadsheet. By generating a list of about 40 interesting prospects, I can whittle this down by further investigating the company's growth potential. This is the next step in the assessment process.

Before we delve into assessing the potential of a particular stock, let's take a look at several stock screening tools that will make your job easier in compiling a list of potential candidates.

5 Stock Screening Tools to Explore:

Here are 5 popular websites that offer free or paid screening tools for the retail stock investor. This is by no means an exhaustive list of tools available online. Take a moment to visit a few of these sites to quickly get a better sense of potential businesses that have solid growth prospects. Without further ado here's the first tool to explore.

(1) *Value Line*.

Value Line offers 25 different paid subscriptions ranging in price from $198 to $1195. The last one is a bit pricey for most investors, wouldn't you say? One option is to check out your local library to see if they carry the newsletter for free.

The Value Line Investment Survey is most famous for its time-tested Ranking Systems for Timeliness, which ranks approximately 1,700 stocks relative to each other for price performance during the next six to 12 months, along with safety. Stocks are ranked from 1 to 5, with 1 being the highest ranking.

(2) *Morningstar*.

Morningstar has one of the best stock screening tools in the market. After signing up for a free account you'll have access to both predefined and custom screens.

The Morningstar 5-Star Rating System for stocks uses a business-centered approach. The rating compares a stock's current price with their analyst's estimate of the stock's fair value. The estimate is based on the present value of the company's future cash flows and does not factor in stock price momentum, investor sentiment or other nonfinancial factors. The Morningstar Rating System identifies stocks that are trading at a discount or at a premium to their fair values.

If you want to tap into the full potential of Morningstar's wealth of research, you'll need to subscribe to Morningstar's Premium Membership Service. You can sign up for a free 2-week trial period on the Morningstar website. Fortunately, many online discount brokers provide access to many of the stock screening tools and reports offered by Morningstar. Check with your online broker to see what might be available.

(3) American Association of Individual Investors.

AAII offers members 3 tiers of subscriptions from $49 to $99 per annum. The purpose of AAII's Stock Screen area is to provide members with access to a wide range of stock strategies and investment approaches. The stock screens are updated monthly and cover over 60 stock investment strategies as well as the companies that pass each screen.

The basic annual membership includes:

- 12 Issues of the *AAII Journal*.
- AAII Model Stock, Mutual Fund, and ETF Portfolios.
- Yearly Tax Planning Guide.

- Access to Local Chapter Meetings.
- And of course, the 60 On-Line Stock Screens.

The American Association of Individual Investors is a non-profit education publisher that has been successfully aiding do-it-yourself investors for over 35 years.

(4) *Yahoo! Finance*.

Yahoo Finance allows you to create your own screens with over 100 different stock screening criteria or filters. This is a good free stock screening tool to use for simple screens. In the beginning, some stock investors feel that their finances are tighter than a belt after Thanksgiving. Going the freebie route when you're just starting out is a good alternative to paid subscription sites, wouldn't you agree?

(5) *The Blue Collar Investor*.

Bar none, this is the next best thing to winning the lottery. The Blue Collar Investor is one of my favorite screening and educational sites for covered call writers. Alan Ellman has been successfully using covered call strategies for over a decade. His premium membership is geared towards the do-it-yourself stock investor wanting to capitalize on using covered call option strategies with market leaders.

You'll receive weekly reports for:

- The top stocks to write (sell) covered calls on.
- The top dividend-producing stocks. and
- The top ETF's with option contracts.

A 1st month premium trial is $19.95 and is $49.95 each month thereafter. This particular tool will shave hours of research off your investing. As well, the stock picks are selected specifically with covered call strategies in mind. Can you imagine what a shortcut this will be to your success?

Badda bing, badda boom! You now have an idea as to where to look for potential opportunities that you could put onto your watchlist. May I suggest that you have some fun exploring the free sites before committing to one or several paid services.

In this chapter, we've explored how to find potential candidates. Now it's time to narrow down your watchlist by looking at assessing the growth potential of each prospect. To do so, I'll share some basic selection criteria to help you assess the viability of your picks.

And if this doesn't make you want to jump up on a bar stool and dance the Macarena, I don't know what will.

~

4

ASSESSING PROFITABILITY

We'll be following three key steps when picking potential stocks for your investment portfolio. This process involves analyzing several businesses to determine which ones have the greatest upside potential for growth. And before committing any of your hard-earned cash to any stock purchase, you'll be doing an in-depth market leader analysis of these businesses. This analysis takes into account the following three steps:

Step #1: Compare the fundamentals of each business over a minimum 5-year period of time. Fundamentals refer to the rate of growth of sales, income, and equity in comparison to the on-going expenses and liabilities of the business. Ideally, you're looking for businesses with a long track record of consistently growing owner/ shareholder equity year over year.

Step #2: Determine the type and extent of the competitive advantage or economic moat that the business has created that sets it apart from its competition. We'll explore seven types of economic moats in a moment.

Step #3: Assess the management's focus and compensation. You're going to be looking for CEO's that are passionate about their work and the importance they place on creating real long-term sustainable value for their shareholders.

Look for management teams that are fairly compensated for their efforts as opposed to the few who rip off unsuspecting shareholders with outrageous bonuses and pay hikes.

I must admit that the identification and assessment of potential stocks can be a tedious process. This is why you should try to use those free or inexpensive tools that make the selection process faster and easier. You may wish to have a pot of coffee handy to help keep your focus sharp.

The extent of research and effort that you'll put in boils down to three factors:

- How much time you have to realistically do your due diligence.
- Whether or not your stock will be held long-term as an investment, such as a dividend-paying stock, or short-term as a cash flow trade as in the case of a monthly covered call.
- Your personal preference as to how much money you could allocate to tap into the speed and convenience offered by subscription sites like The Blue Collar Investor.

My intent in the last chapter was to showcase several stock screening tools thereby giving you some options that you can access. Once you've screened for some potential stock candidates and placed them on your personal watchlist, drill down deeper and assess the quality of each particular opportunity on your own using the assessment criteria described in this chapter or use a paid service that will provide you with some strong possibilities.

I would suggest that every novice investor learn how to use the assessment criteria as part of the overall selection process. Once you understand how each particular factor helps you identify those industry leaders that offer you the greatest upside potential, then you can begin to streamline your selection process. Makes sense, right?

How you go about your selection process is going to depend on two factors. Here's some sage advice to consider:

1. Put more effort into the assessment process as your holding period for your stock increases. If you're looking for a quality dividend-paying stock that you would like to hang onto for at least one year, then take the time to thoroughly check out the holding.
2. Spend more time assessing the upside potential of a particular stock when the reward and risk also increase. For example, a higher option premium often translates into higher volatility and price swings with a stock.

Time to move on to some of the favorite assessment criteria used by many of today's successful stock investors and educators.

Top 9 Assessment Criteria for Market Leaders:

To identify fundamentally sound businesses with upside growth potential, we're going to use just a handful of criteria in the selection process.

The following list of nine criteria is based on what several of the top investment experts have used in their selection process. An overview of these criteria is as follows:

1. Return on invested capital (ROIC) > 10%.
2. Book value per share growth rate (BVPS) > 10%.

3. Earnings per share growth rate (EPS) > 10%.
4. Revenue or sales growth rate > 10%.
5. Cash flow growth rate > 10%.
6. Debt-to-equity ratio (D/E) should be low and preferably < 0.5.
7. Price-to-earning-to-growth ratio (PEG) < 1.0.
8. Price-to-sales ratio (P/S) should be low & < 1.0.
9. Relative strength index (RSI) should be high within a range of 60 to 80 for momentum plays.

All of the five key growth rates should be consistent over a minimum 5-year period. Focus your attention on seeing consistent growth in earnings over a 5 to 7-year period of time, with the capital being generated being put to good use by the management to grow the business.

Let's zoom in and take a look at how each of these nine factors can be used in your assessment process.

5 Key Growth Rates:

In order to confirm the strength of a business, you want to be able to use just a handful of indicators that help you determine whether you can trust and predict that the business can deliver double-digit returns in the future. And, we want to keep the process as simple as possible. Wouldn't you agree?

We also want to be able to compare rates of change as opposed to the raw numbers. Monitoring rates of change goes hand-in-hand with the concept of increasing the speed of your money. Let's look at these popular indicators right now:

(1) Return on Investment Capital (ROIC).

The rate of return a business makes on the cash it invests every year is known as the ROIC. It's helpful in that it is a measure of how effective a company uses its own and borrowed money invested in its operations. A lot of analysts like to place greater weight on this fundamental ratio as it tells you how effective the business is in using invested capital. This ratio is a strong predictor that the business has a competitive advantage in its industry.

(2) *Equity or Book Value per Share Growth Rate (BVPS).*

This metric tells you what the business would be worth if it's no longer a business. The BVPS is the liquidation value or book value of the company. Looking at equity or book value is not helpful as a raw number on its own. It's the rate of equity growth that is key in comparing businesses.

Ideally, look for businesses that are growing their equity over time and not spending excessive funds to build new capital-intensive projects.

(3) *Earnings per Share Growth Rate.*

How much the business is profiting per share of ownership is known as the EPS. You'll find this number along the last line on the business's income statement. Once again, we're more concerned with the growth rate, which you can either quickly calculate on our own or find on financial websites that have this feature.

(4) *Revenue or Sales Growth Rate.*

The total amount of money that the business took in from selling its products and services is used to calculate the revenue or sales growth rate. You'll find the raw number on the top line of the income statement. Profitability is what all businesses are about and tracking revenue growth year-over-year helps with that assessment.

(5) *Free Cash Flow Growth Rate.*

Is the business growing its cash with profits or are these numbers just on paper? This metric is important when the economy takes a turn for the worse. Having actual free cash on hand eliminates the need to borrow excessive amounts of funds.

Ideally, all of the growth rates should be equal to or greater than 10% per year for the last 5, 3 and 1 year. When you have access to several growth rates for comparison, you get a better sense of how the company is growing over a period of time. Look for consistent growth in these numbers over time. We want all the rates going up or at least staying the same.

This is a quick overview of the top 5 growth rates. Self-made stock investment millionaire Phil Town pioneered the approach of using these particular 5 fundamental growth rates to find wonderful businesses at attractive prices. His books Rule 1 and Payback Time provide a detailed step-by-step process for assessing the merits of any stock. Imagine how much easier these resources could make your learning. Something to consider, right?

(6) Debt-to-Equity Ratio.

How much a company owes in relation to how much it owns is known as the debt-to-equity ratio. To arrive at this ratio, simply divide the total liabilities by the net equity. Most financial websites report this metric. What to look for is that it should be low and preferably less than 0.5.

Also look at the company's balance sheet to determine the total amount of debt coming due over the next few years. If there is a great deal of debt, dividends from dividend-paying companies may be slashed in order to ensure paying off any bond holders first.

What I like to do is a quick check to see if the long-term debt of the company can be paid off in less than 3 years with the current free cash flow or net earnings. This gives me a margin of safety in assessing the extent of debt on the company's books.

The ideal scenario is that it should be zero thus enabling the business to readily respond to drastic changes in the economy. However, those businesses capable of paying off debt within a 3-year window are still good prospects to consider.

(7) PEG Ratio.

Use this indicator when you want to compare two or more like businesses together. The PEG is the Price-to-Earnings Multiple (P/E) divided by its earnings growth rate. This metric is an indicator of growth at a reasonable price, or what the stock investment industry calls GARP.

I find the PEG to be helpful in identifying market leaders that are still selling at a good price. The lower the PEG the better, since you're getting more earnings growth for every dollar invested. As a guideline, good prospects have PEG rates less than 1, whereas a PEG rate over 2 is expensive.

Investment guru Peter Lynch who generated an annualized return of 29.8 % from 1977 to 1990 from Fidelity's Magellan Fund while the S&P 500 had an average return of 15.8 % used this metric extensively in his stock selection process. Holy frosted fruit cake! That's impressive.

(8) Price-to-Sales Ratio.

The price-to-sales ratio or PSR is calculated by dividing the stock price per share by the total sales per share. This ratio can help indicate if you are paying too much for the company's stock based on its sales. This is a useful indicator when assessing retailers.

Investment guru Ken Fisher used the price-to-sales ratio in his assessments more so than the price-to-earnings ratio, which he believed can be more volatile.

As a guideline, the lower the PSR the better. Cyclical retailers with a PSR between 0.4 and 0.8 are good investment candidates. Cyclical businesses do better when the economy is doing well, and people have more discretionary money to spend. As well, noncyclical and technology stocks with a PSR between 0.75 and 1.5 also offer good value for investors.

(9) Relative Strength Index.

The RSI is actually a technical indicator of stock momentum and not a fundamental indicator of financial health. This is one technical indicator that'll help you better select stocks that are showing strong growth potential.

The RSI measures the velocity and magnitude of directional price movements in a stock.

The indicator is measured on a scale from 0 to 100, with high and low levels marked at 80 and 20, respectively. Start your initial screening by looking for stocks that have an RSI above 50 and below 80 on the 100-point scale.

So far, so good? This concludes step 1 of your analysis. You now have some assessment tools to incorporate into your overall selection process. Step 2 looks at which businesses have the highest probability of churning out favorable investment returns for years to come. Ready to storm the moat?

7 Economic Moats that'll Help You Make Money:

Besides assessing growth rates, verifying if a business has a well-established economic moat is important.

The term economic moat refers to the idea that the business you're investigating as a potential investment has a long-lasting competitive advantage. The analogy often used is that a moat protects a castle from attack. The wider the moat the easier it is to fend off attackers.

A business with a wide moat is what you want to own long-term. The wider the moat, the more predictable its future five years down the road.

Businesses with a distinctive competitive edge have a degree of predictability. Now correct me if I'm wrong. But having a level of predictability would probably allow you to sleep a little better at night, am I right?

As an investor, look for sustainable and consistent growth rates in key metrics like cash flow, equity and sales over a 3 to 5-year period of time. As cash flow increases so does your profitability and that of the business. With increasing cash flow, a market leader can weather the ups and downs of the economic business cycle paying off debt when needed or investing capital for expanding into new markets.

The following are 7 common types of economic moats to look for in a potential business:

(1) Brand – When you know and trust a particular brand, you'll often pay more for that business's products or services. Disney and Nike are examples of companies that have good brand moats.

(2) Secret - When a business has a patent, copyright or trade secret, it makes competition difficult or illegal. Apple, 3M and Pfizer are examples of corporations with extensive patent portfolios.

(3) Toll - When a business has exclusive control of a market through government approval or licensing, it's able to charge a "toll" for accessing that product or service. Businesses like PG&E, a utility company and Warner Media, a media business owned by AT&T fall into this category.

(4) Switching - When it becomes too much trouble to switch to another provider due to the high monetary and time costs, you've created an economic moat. Both Microsoft and H&R Block are two good examples of companies that benefit from this type of barrier to entry.

(5) Low Price - When products are priced so low no one can compete because they enjoy massive economies of scale due to a huge market share a moat is created. Costco, Home Depot and Wal-Mart all use pricing to establish an economic advantage.

(6) Network Effect - When a business has the ability to quickly dominate a network of end-users by being first in the market, they can often establish an economic advantage. eBay was the first online auction business to dominate the North American market. Amazon also uses its extensive network and distribution system to dominate the online arena.

(7) Unique Corporation Culture - When a business has a way of doing business that would be difficult to duplicate in another business environment or geographical area, you may see an economic moat being established. This was the case when Southwest Airlines established an economic moat in the early years in the airline industry.

And how do you identify an economic moat, you may be asking? Great question, my enthusiastic padawan. The establishment of a viable economic moat manifests itself in the fundamentals that we've previously discussed.

The ideal candidates are businesses that have consistently high growth rates of over 10% per year in return on invested capital, sales, equity and free cash over a period of several years. Hence, the reason why I've described the 5 key fundamentals outlined above. Yes, there is a method to my madness.

Top 4 Mistaken Moats:

Unfortunately, some investors incorrectly mistaken certain characteristics of a business as being some sort of economic advantage. To help keep you out of trouble, here are four mistaken moats to avoid:

(1) Great products.

Just like bad gas, great products come and go, especially if the product is commodity based and can be easily replicated. Having a great product does not ensure that the competition won't arrive on the scene with a newer, sexier, cheaper version. If the consumer can easily switch from one particular product to another, this business may not pan out as a longer-term investment opportunity.

(2) Strong market share.

You may see a business arriving on the scene and dominating a particular market with their product or service. You may even believe that they have somehow created a monopoly. A dominant market share can dwindle rapidly as more competition enters the marketplace. Commodity-based businesses like those that got into the cannabis market early fell into this trap.

(3) Great execution.

Just because a business has an efficient means of doing business doesn't mean that the business has a competitive advantage over the competition. Being efficient is important, but it's not a sustainable advantage unless it's based on some proprietary process that cannot be easily copied. For great execution to be an economic moat that's difficult for the competition to cross, it must show up in the fundamentals over the long haul.

(4) Great management.

Having a shareholder-oriented management team helps to create a wonderful business, but it doesn't constitute being a sustainable advantage. Granted, talented, passionate CEO's do help companies perform better. However, there is no long-term guarantee that a particular individual will stick around after a couple of years.

How often have we seen a stock's price jump in value when new blood comes on board? A word of caution - don't get sucked up in the hype. Short term gains from the jump in the stock price could turn into long-term pains when Mr. Market comes to his senses again.

So far, we've explored how you could use the fundamentals of a business to see how a prospective stock is performing. We've also explored some of the most common economic moats or competitive advantages that sustainable businesses can have. Now, it's time to look at step 3, which is how do we go about checking in on the management team?

Is Management on Your Side?

Step 3 of your assessment process looks at who's running the company. An obvious assumption is that we want the management team to be on the side of the shareholder. Unfortunately, this is not always so. There have been numerous situations where the CEO was being paid hundreds of millions of dollars to run the company into the ground. Yes, you heard me right - being paid hundreds of millions of dollars each year to sit at the helm of the company. I don't know about you, but that scenario makes me madder than a box of frogs.

On a positive note, here are the top four qualities that you want to see in great CEO's:

- Look for a CEO who is service-oriented as opposed to ego-oriented. Their focus should be on serving the owners, the employees, the suppliers, and the customers.

- Great CEO's are passionate about their work and the company they're managing.
- Good CEO's are honorable. They won't tarnish their reputation for power or prestige.
- And great CEO's are driven to change the world for the better. Having big goals, they inspire and motivate the organization they're an integral part of.

And you may be asking, how do you go about finding this information?

Here are five simple ways to check out management without hiring a private eye:

- Type in the CEO's name on Google and read a few online news articles on trade and business sites.
- Check out magazines and newspapers, such as Forbes, Fortune, Barron's, Success, the New York Times and the Wall Street Journal. What's the CEO's reputation in the business community?
- Read the CEO's letter to shareholders and compare the growth rate numbers to what is being said. What's the overall tone of his/her letter? CEO's with integrity will take responsibility for a bad year, admit his or her mistakes and then tell shareholders what he or she intends to do.
- Listen to the CEO's quarterly conference call held with analysts and recorded on the company's website or posted as a transcript of the call. This'll give you insights into the direction the CEO plans to take the company. Don't be fooled into thinking that it's raining outside when the CEO is peeing on your leg.
- Look at recent Insider trading activity on MSN Money, Yahoo Finance or your online broker's website. When company executives are unloading more than 30% of their stock all at

once, this is not a good sign. You can also see if the CEO is getting overpaid through stock options or outrageous perks in addition to their salary. Not what you want to see, am I right?

At every turn, ask yourself, does the business have great Management? You must be confident that the people running the business are doing so as if they intend on being there for decades and not out to rip you off in the short term. Does that sound fair?

Once you've explored a business's fundamentals, competitive advantage and management team you can use the same approach with that business's key competitors to determine who is the true market leader in that industry.

Yes. I do realize that the entire process may be time-consuming at first glance. However, your analysis process will become more streamlined over time. When you do devote a little time to this 3-step process, it'll reward you in the end with some great finds. Not only will your confidence level soar, this will set you up for success when you look into selling covered calls on those market winners. I don't know about you but I'm dancing around Gangnam style. Paws in the air!

As you can see, by identifying and investing initially in only these market leaders across various sectors of the stock market, you increase the likelihood that you'll build up a successful investment portfolio. A little time doing your due diligence ensures that you'll minimize your losses.

As a side note, when you're looking at generating additional income from your holdings, always verify to see if the company in question is also trading in the options market. Ultimately, once you've built up a watchlist of investment possibilities, you're in a position to explore various option strategies that'll generate a consistent stream of relatively passive income into your brokerage account.

Now, all of this in-depth information can be recorded either in a notebook or in an Excel Spreadsheet. Although taking a little more time to set up, a spreadsheet affords the greatest future ease of use for both the calculations and updating information.

This process has served me well in assessing potential candidates. It has helped me streamline the information flow so that I am more efficient, saving me time and a bottle of Tylenol in the process.

Following a set strategy makes your selection and assessment process that much more reliable. There's nothing worse than trying to fart when you have diarrhea. You never know if what's going to come out is poop or air. The same holds true of assessing the merits of individual stocks. Having a step-by-step approach moves you closer to that desired outcome. If you get my drift.

~

5

THE 3 MOST EFFECTIVE COVERED CALL STRATEGIES

You've arrived at the point where we're going to get into the meat of this guide. I know that you didn't fight your way to the top of the food pyramid to become a vegetarian. So, the rest of your book explores various covered call and timing strategies that'll generate higher returns over the long haul. I'm sure that you're rubbing your hands together with all the hope of a newborn fly at a Chinese buffet.

My focus for this particular chapter is to walk you through a handful of popular cash flow strategies for selling covered calls on stock that you own.

But before we delve into the handful of time-tested strategies, let's quickly look at the obvious challenge many do-it-yourself investors are faced with, which is picking the best strategy to use.

A plethora of popular investment strategies exist in the stock market today. Most experts and well-known investment authors have a strong bias towards a particular strategy that better sells their services or investment products. It's very challenging to get an unbiased opinion about a particular investment strategy. Who do you really trust when many of them have hidden agendas?

A key take-away about making money in the stock market is to stick to a proven strategy over time. Just because Plan A fails, doesn't mean you've got 25 more letters to choose from. The longer you work your specific strategy through good times and bad, the more you'll be able to fine tune your outcomes. Let's jump into those three covered call strategies that'll be more than enough to allow you to make a killing in the markets.

3 Effective Covered Call Strategies:

Unlike you, most stock investors are limited to making money only when the stock goes up in price. Whether you're investing long-term or trading stocks every few months as opportunities present themselves, the average investor can only realistically expect a historical market return of 10%.

When we look at the real estate market, an investor can buy property with the hope that it will increase in value over time. This basic concept is no different from the stock investor buying stock in the hopes that it too will go up in value.

Should they choose, a real estate investor can create a monthly cash flow by renting out his or her property. In exchange for providing shelter, the real estate investor is paid rent on a monthly basis.

A similar opportunity is available to the stock investor who can rent out his or her stock in the form of covered call options. The call writer - that's you - would receive cash up front in exchange for the right of the buyer who put up the cash to buy the stock should it reach an agreed upon price.

As a covered call writer, your ability to generate an additional income stream under varying market conditions is available to you. There are three scenarios that you can tap into. The first is when the markets are trending upward, which is when the market is bullish.

Here, you make money when the stock goes up to an agreed upon selling price or what is known as the strike price. You'll often capture both the option premium and any stock price appreciation between your initial price and the strike price.

In the second scenario, you can make money when the stock goes nowhere by capturing just the option premium. This occurs when the markets or the stock are neutral or flat over a period of time. Despite the market or stock not appreciating in value, you're able to still generate a monthly stream of income. Not a bad scenario, wouldn't you say?

And in the third scenario, you can protect your investment better should the stock experience a slight drop in price over the course of a month or so. When the stock market is trending lower, which is a bearish market, selling covered calls offers some downside protection of your stock price. The option premiums that you receive, lower your initial cost basis for the stock. In other words, the premiums that are deposited into your brokerage account actually lower the purchase price of your stock. This third scenario provides you with a slight cushion against loss of capital.

As you can see, the selling of covered calls, increases your ability to generate additional cash flow from your investments. So, how much can you expect to make from writing covered calls? The sweet spot that most experienced call writers shoot for is a monthly premium in the range of 2 to 3% in addition to any stock price appreciation. Given that you could realistically expect to sell monthly calls almost every month that equates to an annual potential total return in excess of 20%. Wouldn't that be better than a kick in the pants with a frozen boot?

Which brings us to the point of learning a few strategies that'll allow you to consistently capture those gains. The purpose of the following section is to do just that - provide you with three simple covered call strategies that you can use to create an income stream from stock investing. But, before we get into the nitty gritty of selling covered calls, let's take a look at a few concepts that you should be familiar with in order to better understand how you can use each of these strategies.

4 Option Conditions:

There are four conditions that you'll need to fill in before your order is fulfilled with your online discount broker when you sell an option contract on stock that you own.

These four requirements are:

(1) The strike price.

This is the price that you agree to sell your stock at should the price of the stock reach this specific price at any time before the contract expires. This means that your shares of stock could be sold at any time the stock price is at or higher than your agreed upon strike price.

Most of the time, the sale of your shares, what is called <u>assignment</u> or <u>exercising your shares</u>, happens on the last day of the contract known as <u>expiration Friday</u>. Expiration Friday is always the 3rd Friday of the expiration month.

Now, the strike price that you select can be above, at or below the current price of the stock. When the strike price is above the current price, the call option is known as an *out-of-the-money* call or OTM. When the strike price is at the current price, it is known as an *at-the-money* call or ATM. And when the strike price is below the current price, it is known as an *in-the-money* call or ITM. We'll look at how each of these relationships fits into our three simple covered call strategies in a moment.

(2) The contract expiration date.

As can be expected, each option contract has a limited life expectancy that is stipulated as the contract expiration date. You being the seller of the options contracts has an advantage especially when the contract period is short as in a 1-month time frame.

The most successful covered call writers prefer working with monthly contracts. This is because of the relationship between contract duration and value. As time passes there is a natural erosion of the value of an options contract, which eventually falls to zero at the end of the trading day on expiration Friday.

(3) The number of contracts.

All option contracts are packaged and sold in whole number lots. Each individual contract controls 100 shares of stock. No fractional units or shares of stock are allowed. For example, let's say you have 470 shares of Babba Gump stock. The maximum number of covered call contracts that you can sell is four. You're unable to write a contract for the remaining 70 shares.

Hence, the reason why you should try to purchase stock in a company in round lots of 100 shares so that you can optimize your option positions. Makes sense, right?

(4) The premium price.

As soon as you sell an option contract, you're paid up front with the cash premium being deposited directly into your brokerage account. The total premium that you receive as a call seller is composed of two parts - time and intrinsic value. To illustrate this concept, here are three simplified call-selling scenarios.

Scenario 1:

If you sold an at-the-money (ATM) call option contract for $2 with a strike price of $60 with the current stock price at $60, your premium paid would be made up of $2 of time value and nothing else. This time value is solely based on the appreciation potential of the option contract. It takes into consideration both the time left until contract expiration and the volatility of the stock as it trades.

Scenario 2:

The same situation holds true should you sell an out-of-the-money (OTM) call. Recall that an out-of-the-money call is a call option whereby the strike price is above the current price of the stock. Once again, it would be made up only of time value and nothing else. Your total premium paid to you would be made up of only the potential for option appreciation by a specified date. And this premium would get smaller the further out-of-the-money you sell your option contract for. For example, you might only receive $1 for a strike price of $62, instead of $2 for the $60 strike in the first scenario.

Scenario 3:

Now let's assume in a third scenario that you purchase an in-the-money (ITM) call with a strike of $58 when the stock price is $60, and you receive a premium of $4. Notice that the option contract is now worth $2 more than the at-the-money call in Scenario 1. It has increased in value from $2 to $4, when we looked at our initial ATM call.

This extra $2 that makes up the total premium is attributed to intrinsic value. Intrinsic value just tells you if the option has any true or real value. It's related to how much a particular option is in-the-money giving us some actual tangible value. In this case, the call option is now $2 in-the-money.

The further in-the-money the option is the greater it's intrinsic value. This value is approximately equal to the number of dollars that the stock price is in-the-money. Following me so far?

Of course, this is an over-simplification of the premium calculation process. However, it does illustrate the relationship between time and intrinsic value.

To recap, the four basic parameters that you'll need to initially input when you login to your online brokerage account for selling a covered call contract are:

- The strike price.
- The contract expiration date.
- The number of option contracts.
- The premium price.

So, how do you go about placing a covered call order?

I'll cover this process in detail in Chapter 6 but for now here's an overview of the process you'll be following:

- Just head on over to your online discount brokerage account and login.
- Once you've identified the stock holding that you own, open up the option chain for the stock. The option chain is just a list or menu of option strike prices with the corresponding premiums.
- Place a "limit" order that is good for the day for your option order rather than sending the order in as a "market" order. By placing a limit price for your orders, you have greater control over the price you could end up initially selling your contracts at. Then, you're pretty much done. Easy peasy, right?

Now that you have an idea as to which parameters you need to enter for each call option position you undertake, let's take a look at the three simple call selling strategies to place in your investment arsenal.

Please keep in mind that these strategies are not carved in stone. As with any strategy, they're to be used as a guideline in helping you make the best investment choices that'll help you create monthly cash flow and provide some protection of your capital.

Stock markets tend to trend upwards over time. Let's start by taking a look at how you can further tap into this trend with stocks that are showing some price appreciation.

The Growth Generation Strategy:

When the stock market is trending higher, you can capture gains from the stock price appreciation, as well as the premium you receive from selling your calls. This strategy works best under the following four conditions:

Condition #1: The stock and the market as a whole are experiencing an upward bullish trend with low volatility.

This information can be seen on a technical chart of both a broad-based index such as the S&P 500 and a technical chart of the stock being analyzed. Take a look at the stock's price and trading volume over several months of graphed data points. I like to use the free charting tools found at StockCharts.com.

When looking at a technical chart of the S&P 500 Index the overall market should be appreciating over the time frame selected. A graph is visual in nature and is easier for you to identify patterns that have unfolded in a particular stock. Makes a lot of sense, right?

Condition #2: Next, while still looking at a technical chart, assess the 200-day and 50-day simple moving-day averages to see if they are moving in a positive direction on high volume. The moving day average is a popular technical indicator that shows the value of a stock over a specific time period.

Many stock investors use moving averages to tell them about the direction the stock's price may be headed. In general, look for the moving-day averages of the market to be trending higher with this particular strategy.

The other part to the equation is to see if the market and the stock are trading on above average volume. High volume equates to confidence in the stock and the underlying business. Trading volume tells you whether or not investors are putting their money on the line in the stock market.

Condition #3: While looking at the technical chart, assess whether or not the positive momentum of the stock price is relatively continuous and not a spike. An ideal situation is to see the price appreciation of the stock occurring gradually over a recent 3 to 6-month block of time.

There are two other technical indicators to consider using in conjunction with moving-day averages. They are the MACD and the Relative Strength Index or RSI.

Here's a simple description of each of these technical indicators:

The MACD:

The MACD or Moving Average Convergence Divergence is a momentum indicator that helps determine when a trend has ended or begun and may reverse direction.

The MACD is composed of two moving average lines and a zero line. The solid black line is called the MACD line and the slower moving red or dotted line is the signal line. When the MACD line crosses above the signal line and the zero line this indicates a positive trend in the market.

Rather than get caught up in trying to interpret what the lines are doing, look at a histogram representation of the indicator to graphically tell you when a trend is reversing. The default setting for the MACD is 12, 26, 9. You may wish use a more sensitive setting of 8, 17, 9.

The RSI:

The relative strength index or RSI helps to determine if an individual stock has been oversold or overbought by investors. I mentioned this indicator briefly in the last chapter.

The RSI is an oscillator that moves between 0 and 100. When the RSI rises above 70 or 80, it's a signal that the stock is overbought and money may begin to flow out of the stock causing a price decline. On the flip side, when the RSI falls below 30 or 20, it's a signal that the stock is oversold and investors may be enticed to buy the stock, which causes the stock price to rise.

It's best to use the RSI with individual stocks, as opposed to the market as a whole, and with a short-term time frame such as a few weeks. It becomes a useful tool for any do-it-yourself investor. Stocks with a rising RSI above 50 and below 80, fall into our sweet spot for potential growth candidates.

Condition #4: The fourth condition to incorporate into your decision-making process is to determine if the stock is in a strong industry. Industries tend to go in and out of favour with the big institutional buyers.

Often the popularity of a specific industry or sector is heavily influenced by current global and economic trends. Stocks that are in favour with Mr. Market have an easier time of seeing appreciating stock prices.

Various free informational websites and even your online discount broker may have a news feed that portrays how various economic sectors are doing in the stock market. A quick check will help you assess the direction that these sectors are heading in and whether or not the stock you've selected has upward growth potential.

Advantages of the Growth Generation Strategy.

The three major advantages of using the growth generation strategy are that:

- When you set up an out-of-the-money call, you profit from both the option premium received and the upside appreciation of the stock.
- You decrease the chance of your stock being assigned and called away (in other words cashed out) at the end of the option cycle since the stock price has further to rise than an at-the-money call option.
- You benefit from time decay working in your favour since there is no intrinsic value, only time value. As time lapses, the value of the option premium approaches zero, accelerating even faster a few days before expiration Friday.

Disadvantages of the Growth Generation Strategy.

The top three disadvantages are that:

- This strategy produces the least amount of downside protection should the stock decline in value. This is because there is no intrinsic value should you have sold an in-the-money call.
- You also receive an initial premium that is low. The further away the strike price is from the current stock price the lower the premiums. At-the-money calls yield you the highest "initial" premiums.
- You could pay more to close your position should the stock price drop. This is due to the relationship between stock price

and option price known as Delta.

Delta is known as the <u>hedge ratio</u> and is defined as the amount an option price will change given a 1-point change in the price of the stock. It tells you the relationship between a stock and option's price movement.

For call options, Delta values range from 0 to 1. If for example a stock moves up 2 points and the option Delta happens to be 1 or 100%, the option will also move up 2 points.

Deep in-the-money calls show this relationship where an increase or decrease in the stock price is almost equal dollar for dollar with an increase in the option price. As a rule of thumb, a stock that is at-the-money (ATM), meaning that its price is at or near the option's strike price will have a Delta of approximately 0.5 on the zero to 1 scale.

As the stock's price drops the Delta approaches zero. In other words, there's less movement in the price of the option in relation to the stock price the further it drops.

So, why should I care, you may be asking? The Delta provides you with a means to compare the interaction between the stock and option pricing for a particular stock. When using a growth strategy, it's often more expensive to close your option position as the stock price declines, which may limit your profitability on the contract.

What's important to know is that option's pricing is dynamic since the erosion of time has an impact on pricing especially as one approaches expiration and all options contracts fall to zero.

Holy pretzel, Batman! I've probably overwhelmed you with that fancy schmancy stuff about Delta. And I may be contributing to your hair loss. When your head ceases spinning like a whirling dervish, take a deep breath before reading on.

To best illustrate this growth strategy in action let's use an example to show you step-by-step how you might structure a growth play.

(1) Growth Generation in a Bull Market.

You've been looking at a technical chart of the stock Crusty Crabb Pizza, symbol CRAB, which over the past couple of months has been showing positive growth signs. This was confirmed by the upward movement of the stock price with both the 200-day and 50-day moving averages.

With further investigation you notice that Crusty Crabb Pizza has recently traded with above average volume. It has a relative strength index that is above 50 and below 80. You also notice that the MACD indicator is above the horizontal zero line indicating that momentum in the stock is positive.

You determine that you have a number of positive signals that allow you to better execute an option growth strategy.

Now you need to take a look at the various option prices and select an appropriate strike price that'll hopefully give you a monthly return of 2 to 3% - your sweet spot.

It's now time to check out what the profit potential is for a couple of call options. A simple way to determine which strike price meets your profit objective is to plug the four key parameters we previously discussed for option's trading into the Ellman calculator, which can be downloaded from The Blue Collar Investor for free. Or, you could create a similar one yourself using an electronic spreadsheet.

To assess the profitability of various strike prices, log into your online discount broker's website that lists the various call option strike prices. You'll need to enter onto your spreadsheet:

- The strike price of the two options just "above" the current price of the stock.
- The dollar value of the two option premiums.
- The price you paid for the stock initially (or will pay) and the number of shares purchased. Remember we ideally want round lots of 100 so that we can sell one option contract per 100 shares of stock owned.
- The number of option contracts you would like to sell. Ideally shoot for 4 to 5 contracts so as to minimize the effects of transaction fees.

Let's assume that the initial stock price was $33.00 and that there were two strike prices just above the stock price.

The lower strike price of 34 was going to give you a premium of $1.00 from the sale producing an immediate option return of 3.0%, while a higher strike of 36 gives you $0.50 for an option return of 1.5%.

Each strike price is multiplied by 100 to arrive at the amount of premium deposited into your brokerage account for every contract that you sell. These dollar values would be immediately deposited into your account once Mr. Market finds a specific buyer. This is all set this up seamlessly behind the scenes.

To recap what these two scenarios would provide is that you would receive $100 for every option contract sold at a strike of 34 and $50 for every option contract sold at the higher strike of 36. Recall that you control 100 shares of stock therefore the premium listed is multiplied by a factor of 100 in order to arrive at the actual amount of premium deposited directly into your brokerage account. So far, so good?

Your maximum potential total return based on the option premium received plus the maximum stock appreciation that you could realize gives you a potential of 6.0% for the lower strike price of 34 and 10.6% for the higher strike of 36.

Please keep in mind that these are hypothetical maximum returns based on the notion that your stock will appreciate in value up to the strike price and be <u>called away</u>. The term called away refers to your stock being sold at the strike price. Once sold you would benefit from the appreciated value of the stock and the option premium being paid initially. Not a bad 1-month return by any means, wouldn't you say?

Your decision as to which opportunity is going to get you closer to your objectives should place a greater weight on how much of a premium you could receive up front versus what the potential might be if the stock appreciates in price.

As a rule of thumb, select a higher strike price for stocks that you plan on holding for more than one month. For example, a higher strike price makes sense if you have a dividend-paying stock from which you would like to generate some additional monthly cash flow.

If you're not partial to the stock, then selecting a lower strike price with a richer up-front premium may make more sense for your income generation.

After you've assessed the income potential for each scenario using your spreadsheet, you'll then place your <u>sell-to-open</u> order on your online brokerage trading platform. You'll be placing a limit order between the bid and ask prices for the option, rather than a market order. The limit price provides greater control over the actual price you'll receive in option premiums.

The bid price that you see in the option chain represents the suggested price that buyers are willing to pay for that particular option strike price. The bid price is always lower than the ask price for a particular option.

The ask price is the suggested price that sellers like you are willing to sell their option contract at to a willing buyer. You'll often find yourself selling your options contracts somewhere between the lower bid price and midway between the bid and ask spread.

Let's move on to the next option strategy that of income generation in primarily neutral markets.

The Income Generation Strategy:

The primary goal of an income strategy for call options is to capture high premiums from your call selling. This strategy works best under the following three conditions:

Condition #1: The stock you're analyzing and the stock market as a whole are trading sideways or flat with little or no price appreciation. Also, trading is occurring with an average volume of transactions.

Condition #2: The 200-day and 50-day simple moving-day averages are leveling out and may be converging. This can be a good predictor that the stock in question or the market as a whole are cooling off.

Condition #3: The technical indicators such as MACD and RSI are not giving any clear buy or sell signals. They may be relatively flat.

When the stock and the market as a whole are meeting these conditions, an income strategy for call options may be opportune.

Advantages of the Income Generation Strategy.

An income generation strategy has predominantly two major advantages:

- It provides the highest initial option return resulting in a pure income generation play.
- And, it takes advantage of maximizing immediate cash flow into your brokerage account.

Disadvantages of the Income Generation Strategy.

The downside of using the income generation strategy is that:

- You have no upside potential for stock price appreciation. Typically, you'll be selling option contracts with a strike price at or close to your stock price, in other words at-the-money.
- With an in-the-money call position, you have downside protection generated from both the intrinsic value and call premium you'll receive. An at-the-money call limits your protection to just the amount of premium received.
- You have a high probability of the stock being called away. Your holding will be sold with the proceeds being deposited into your brokerage account. Not a great strategy to use with a dividend stock or one that you plan on holding long-term.

(2) Income Generation in a Flat Market.

Let's assume you purchased Crusty Crabb Pizza when the stock was trading at $30. Looking at a technical chart of the stock, you see that this stock has been trading sideways for quite some time with little fluctuation. You also notice that for the past 2 months trading volume has been average.

Upon further observation, you see that the 50-day moving average is virtually flattening out and both the 200-day and 50-day moving averages are converging and moving closer to each other. This often can signal that an upward trend is coming to an end. You also observe that the relative strength index is hovering around 50 giving you no clear buy or sell signals. And the same situation pans out for the MACD indicator.

With an income generation strategy, you want to capture the highest call option premium possible knowing that in all likelihood your stock will be called away on or before expiration Friday and that your potential profit will be derived solely from the call premium.

Although you may question the sanity of this strategy with having your stock called away and sold, you do profit from the options trade. Recall, that you're attempting to structure your call options so that you generate a conservative monthly option return of 2 to 3%.

Imagine where you would be if you were to rinse and repeat this one strategy over the course of a year.

As previously mentioned, your potential returns could exceed 20%. I don't know about you, but this would make me happier than the monks who discovered the word was "celebrate" not "celibate".

Here's how you'll set up this little cash generation opportunity in your brokerage account. First, log into your broker's website that lists the various call option strike prices for Crusty Crabb Pizza. We want to assess the profitability of the closest option strike prices to the current stock price.

You'll then add the following info into your spreadsheet:

- The strike prices of the "closest" one or two options to the current price of the stock. In this case $30.
- The dollar value of the one or two option premiums.
- The price you initially paid for the stock and the number of shares purchased. Recall that we want round lots of 100 so that we can sell one option contract per 100 shares of stock owned.

- And finally, the number of option contracts you would like to sell.

Let's assume a strike price of 30 gives you $0.90 from the sale producing an immediate return of approximately 3%. Each option contract sold immediately generates $90.

This is the maximum expected return on your investment. You won't benefit from any upside growth potential of the stock price appreciating. In contrast, you do capitalize on the maximum premium value associated with the calls since they are at-the-money.

If on expiration Friday, Crusty Crabb Pizza traded above $30 your option contracts would have been exercised and the shares sold at $30. A 1-month return of approximately 3% would be in your brokerage account and you're now free to enter into another profitable opportunity.

Your actual return will be slightly less than 3% because fees associated with selling the option contract need to be accounted for. When you sell 4 or 5 contracts at a time the fees have less of an impact on your returns.

Hence, the reason why you want to work with a discount broker and group your option contracts together. Following the paper trail so far?

The Protection Strategy:

With a protection strategy for call options, you'll be capturing premiums from your call selling as well as cushioning your cash basis in your stock should the stock price decline slightly over the course of the month.

This strategy works best under the following four conditions:

Condition #1: Both the stock and the market are experiencing a slightly downward or bearish trend with a volatile market tone. Volatility shows up when you see large swings on a technical chart with a stock's price or with the market in general.

Condition #2: On a technical chart, the graph of the 50-day simple moving-day average has crossed under the 200-day moving average moving in a negative direction.

Condition #3: You're seeing mixed technical indicators for the equity you're analyzing. Nothing definitive can be derived from the RSI or MACD indicators.

Condition #4: Also consider using this strategy in an up-trending chart pattern when there is increased volatility in the markets.

Advantages of the Protection Strategy.

There are three key advantages of using the protection strategy:

- As expected, you'll receive immediate option profit from the sale of the call.
- The premiums received create downside protection for your stock price by lowering the cost basis of the purchase price for your holding.
- This particular strategy has lower risk compared to the other two call option strategies.

Disadvantages of the Protection Strategy.

The top three disadvantages are that:

- You have no upside potential. The strike price selected will most likely be at or lower than the current price of the stock.

- Since you do not participate in any potential for share appreciation, there are lost opportunity costs.
- You have a high probability of the stock being called away on or before expiration Friday.

(3) Protection in a Declining Market.

Let's assume that you purchased Crusty Crabb Pizza at a stock price of $39. Soon after, the stock experienced a slightly bearish (negative) trend as evidenced by the 50-day simple moving-day average crossing under the 200-day moving average moving in a negative direction.

Both the MACD and relative strength index were showing short-term mixed signals. The RSI was floating above and below 50. And, the MACD momentum indicator had been moving above and below the zero line every couple of weeks.

If you're going to take a bearish outlook on this particular stock, then look at strike prices that are below the current price of the stock. Your primary goal would be to build in some downside protection for the price of the stock to decline slightly during the course of the month.

Start, by logging into your online broker's website and look at the various call option strike prices for the current month. You'll need to enter onto your spreadsheet the following information:

- The strike price of the closest two options just "below" the current price of the stock. Ideally, you're looking for strike prices with high Delta values above 90%.
- The dollar value of the two option premiums.
- The price you paid for the stock initially and the number of shares purchased.
- The number of option contracts you would like to sell.

Let's say that from these two scenarios the lowest strike price of 35 gives you $4.20 from the option sale producing an immediate cash deposit of 10.8%, while the higher strike of 37.50 gives you a cash premium of $2.00 for an immediate cash deposit of 5.1%.

Let's take a look at the downside protection created by this strategy. In the first case, the lowest selected strike price of 35 reduces your cost basis for the stock from $39 to $34.80, which is roughly calculated by subtracting your premium received from your stock price. In order for this position to lose money the stock price would have to drop below this level.

In the second scenario with the higher strike price of 37.50, you're able to reduce your cost basis of the stock from $39 to $37 which gives you 5.1% of downside protection.

Both strikes have some time value that you can profit from should the stock remain above the strike price of the call options all the way to expiration.

With the lower strike of 35 you have 20 cents of time value premium (35.00 strike - $34.80 cost basis). You would capture this time value premium should the stock be exercised and called away. The 20 cents would give you a 0.5% monthly return. Not much in the way of a return, wouldn't you say?

However, the purpose of this particular strategy is for the downside protection that it offers in a slightly down trending market and not for income generation.

On the flip side, the higher strike of 37.50 has 50 cents of time value giving you a potential monthly return of 1.3%. The intrinsic value for this particular strike was calculated by subtracting the 37.50 strike price from the current stock price of 39 giving you 2.50. And the time value is the difference between the 2.00 in intrinsic value and the total premium of 2.50 leaving you with the 50 cents.

At this point of your calculations, your final decision becomes, how much protection you need versus immediate cash generated.

Keep in mind, this strategy works best with declining stock prices that are temporary in nature. The market will eventually trend higher. Using the protection strategy in an upward trending steady market will in all likelihood produce losses.

Now that you have a brief idea as to how you could use covered calls for three specific investment situations, it's time to look at some totally trippin tips. Ready?

Top Five Covered Call Strategy Tips:

Time to pass on some sage advice. Here are five of my favorite strategy tips for writing covered calls on stock that you own.

(1) Use a variety of options strategies, not just one.

Base your option strategy decisions on the direction and mood of the market. Just because selling out-of-the-money calls is one of the most popular option strategies, doesn't mean that you should neglect or avoid the other two.

(2) Watch the greed factor.

Want to be caught with your pants down around your ankles? Avoid selling covered calls that generate excessively high monthly returns. Your sweet spot for monthly returns should be in the range of 2 to 3%; anything higher than 5% may be a sign of higher stock volatility and risk.

(3) Take full responsibility for your decisions.

Don't blame your neighbour's pet hamster or Mr. Market for the outcome of a particular investment decision. Every potential investment opportunity is unique. Learn from the mistakes that you'll inevitably make, but do not dwell on the negative outcome. All great investors make errors that cost them money. How else are they going to learn what works or doesn't for them?

Your goal should be to reduce the number of errors that you can control yourself over time. Re-focus your energy and time looking for the next potential opportunity. When you look at the market as being the enemy, you take yourself out of the constant flow of opportunities that present themselves. By freeing up your mind you can now focus on moving into and out of better and better opportunities.

(4) If you're emotionally upset, in a euphoric mood or under above average stress from your work/ home environment, avoid placing a trade.

When your emotional state is out of whack with your normal operating state, you tend to make silly mistakes that'll cost you money in the end. By tuning into your emotional state prior to each trade, you'll be able to increase your ability to consistently place winning trades, while minimizing or eliminating common trading errors completely. To help you with this process, check out the resources listed in the appendix.

(5) Optimize don't maximize each trade.

It's okay for you to leave money on the table. Just know that opportunities present themselves every month. Trying to maximize your profits also increases your risk level. Stay within your comfort zone of risk tolerance. You'll be a much happier camper in doing so.

Now that you have some sage advice as to how to implement the three key call option strategies, let's explore when you should enter and exit positions.

~

6

ENTERING & EXITING POSITIONS

I n this particular chapter, you'll be discovering a variety of timing strategies for moving into and out of stock and option positions in order to optimize your profitability.

Contrary to what you may have heard about investors not being able to time the market, you can learn to be more adept at entering and exiting positions so that you increase the probability of coming out on top.

One of the most frustrating aspects of stock investing is trying to figure out when you should move into and out of positions. It often takes years of research and hands on experience to figure out what time periods you should avoid based on the documented historical trends.

It's true that you will in all likelihood not be able to time the market tops and bottoms, thus enabling you to maximize your profits. No one has been able to do this in a consistent manner in the stock market.

You can however take advantage of certain times of the day, week, month or year to enable you to better optimize your profits. The timing strategies shared in this chapter will help you create your "edge" thereby increasing your profitability potential in the stock market. Ready to tap into some tips?

Here are my top timing tips that'll help you better time entering and exiting the market. And more importantly, I'll explain why each of these tips is appropriate.

(1) Avoid buying stock or call options on a Monday.

Mondays tend to produce higher than normal price volatility throughout the day. A case in point is the massive sell-off and panic that ensued in the markets on Monday, March 9, 2020.

Often professional traders arrive back at work on Monday morning in a less than desirable mood. Markets tend to trade more on emotions than on rational assessment throughout the day on Mondays. This is not where you want to be as the markets seesaw back and forth between negative and positive territory.

You're better off ignoring what's occurring in the markets on Mondays. Wait for the markets to play out during the course of the day. They can be emotionally charged after the weekend.

(2) Trade on Wednesdays and Thursdays.

So, when would be the ideal time to try to better time your market plays? Mid-week often presents better opportunities than either the beginning or end of the week. Historically, Wednesday's have produced the most gains since 1990.

For many big institutional players Fridays tend to be a day for unloading certain positions before the weekend.

These big players would rather not hold onto potentially volatile stocks that may be affected by news over the weekend.

You should also be aware of the fact that many institutional traders take off early on Friday afternoon. This means that the smaller players become the temporary price movers.

To avoid being caught with your pants down, verify if the price movement of the stock is in synch with the volume of shares being traded. Should you see a rising stock price, yet the volume is decreasing, this is a signal that the current stock price trend is unsustainable over time.

(3) Avoid trading when the stock market opens or during the lunch hour.

Wait at least an hour or so after the opening bell before getting into the market. Don't make my mistake by overpaying for a position.

Midday is another problematic time of the day. With a lot of institutional traders taking their lunch during the lunch hour there are fewer traders and market volume tends to lag.

Be patient my little padawan. See how the day is unfolding in the markets. It could save you a few bucks in the end. By waiting until the end of the day when volume is typically the heaviest, you may be in a better position to assess your timing opportunity.

Keep in mind that above average volume with rising stock prices is a signal that investors are confident in a particular stock or the market as a whole.

(4) Avoid trading near the end of a quarter.

Stocks that have been lack lustre over the past quarter need to be monitored closely. Often institutional players unload poor performers so that they can re-balance their overall portfolio. The mutual fund industry is very competitive. Many fund managers take a short-term approach to investing in order to hang onto their client's money.

Near the end of each quarter assess the impact of buying or selling particular holdings based on what you feel the big boys may be doing. Many successful investors get a feel for the tone of the market as a whole by watching how money is flowing into the stock market versus the bond market or commodities markets such as gold and oil. Try to use the same tactic.

(5) Avoid trading when company earnings are announced.

You'll often see volatile stock price movement during the time period just leading up to and shortly after an earnings report release. Earnings reports often cause shifts in momentum and valuations. Should you be selling covered calls on the stock during the same month that earnings are going to be announced, expect a roller coaster ride.

Your best bet is to wait out the period around the earnings report release to see how the stock market will react to the information rather than commit yourself to a call position. Capital preservation is key. By sidestepping the option's market for one month you can always take up a position once you're assured that the news won't have a negative effect on that holding.

(6) Avoid trading right after big announcements.

Government announcements and major economic events do have the power to move the markets. Here's a short list of regularly scheduled events that you could keep your eye on:

- The ISM Manufacturing Index from the Institute for Supply Management: An index above 50 indicates a growing economy.
- The US Unemployment Report from the Department of Labor measures how tight the labor market is.
- The 10-Year T-Note Auction from the U.S. Treasury: Use this to track investor movement in/out of stocks.

- The Retail Sales Report from the Department of Commerce measures consumer spending which helps predict economic growth.
- The Existing Home Sales Report from the National Association of Realtors shows housing market trends.
- The China Purchasing Management Index provides a good picture of global manufacturing health.

This list is by no means exhaustive. The economic data provided by these 1/2 dozen announcements can sometimes help you develop a better edge in the markets. A lot of these announcements can be seen being summarized on mainstream TV.

(7) Be cautious during the first 2 weeks of January.

Year-end earnings announcements in early January can result in increased stock price volatility.

This is also the period of time that many institutional players re-balance their entire portfolios for the upcoming year. You'll often see increased price volatility at the start of the New Year. Better to wait on the sidelines until the big boys have finished their dance so that you don't overpay on any one position.

(8) Schedule any important moves after mid-April.

It's tax time. US stock markets tends to be more prone to weakness after the mid-month tax deadline in the Excited States. Some of this disruption is due to individual investor money moving out of the markets in order to pay for tax obligations owing. It's also a period of time when some investors rebalance their portfolios in order take advantage of certain capital losses.

You may want to hold off any major moves that could have an impact on your current tax liabilities owing. Check with a financial planner or accountant prior to making any such big moves.

(9) Be cautious investing in early October.

Historically, the beginning of October has often been weak for the stock market. You may notice that there are fewer growth plays during this particular time period. The markets do ramp up for the Christmas season, but this usually occurs in early November.

Don't Fall for This:

When the news is abuzz with all sorts of claims that company XYZ is going to be the next Apple or Amazon, be wary of investing in this stock. This can be tough advice to follow. It's emotionally counter-intuitive to not jump on the investing bandwagon when everyone else is singing praise for a specific stock. While looking for potential stock candidates your judgment can be clouded and influenced by what you see and hear in the news media or from your Uber driver for that matter.

When this situation presents itself - and it will at some point in your investment journey - you're best served by following a specific decision-making process. The 3-step selection process for finding market leaders with growth potential has been discussed in detail in this guide. You've been shown how taking just a handful of key business fundamentals along with a technical chart and some indicators helps you select profitable holdings for the long-term.

Step back and take the time to process the basic data that really matters in executing your specific investment strategy. You'll save yourself a lot of grief and heartache knowing that you haven't been duped by the investo-tainment hype.

Something to consider asking yourself when you see excessive posturing for a particular stock in the media is:

"What are other investors thinking about regarding this recent news and how are they going to react to the recent media attention?"

When I place myself in the shoes of other investors, I'm in a better position to build my edge and increase the probability of making money from any opportunity.

How to Place an Option Sell Order:

Before actually placing your option sell order, you'll need to select one of the three option strategies previously discussed. Then, you'll need to log into your brokerage account to check out the option premiums available. Since you'll be selling monthly calls, look at the option chain for only the specific month you'll be selling calls in. Recall that the option chain contains a list of option strike prices and corresponding premiums from which you'll make your choices.

Always do an initial calculation of the option returns of those 2 or 3 strike prices closest to the current price of the stock. This gives you greater clarity as to the profitability potential of at least a couple of strike prices. It may also give you insights into whether or not the option strategy that you've selected is the most appropriate one.

When looking at the option chain, check out the current bid price, which is the lower price listed in the option chain. Recall, that this is the price buyers are willing to pay for that option contract. Do so for each option strike price. A quick mental calculation will give you a feel for the potential premium you might receive.

When you actually place your sell order, select a strike price that is between the bid and mid-price for that option. The mid-price is the price halfway between the bid and ask prices. If your brokerage platform doesn't post the mid-price - no worries - you can simply do the math in your head or "guestimate" the mid price.

Place the strike prices, corresponding bid prices and your stock price paid onto an option analysis spreadsheet. A simple spreadsheet can quickly calculate the immediate return that you'll generate from the sale of your option contracts.

As an alternative, here's a simplified way of determining the return on your option. You calculate the return on your option by dividing the premium received by the cost basis of your stock. Let me explain with an example.

Should you sell an in-the-money option for some downside protection, the intrinsic value (i.e. protection) is deducted from the option premium before calculating the return. For example, if the stock option is $2 and the stock price is $100, your return on option is: $2/ ($100-$2) = 2.04%.

Once you've determined the return on each of your options, decide which option strike price you'll sell. Simply log into your brokerage account and select the specific option that you would like to sell. Then, enter the number of contracts, followed by a "sell to open" limit order good for the day at a price between the bid and mid prices for the option. Click on the order placement button. And check your order status in several minutes.

Once your broker executes the order, the contracts will be sold, and the premiums deposited immediately into your brokerage account. Take a moment to record the actual premium that you received in either a trading diary or in a spreadsheet that will track your positions.

Should your sell order not be filled as quickly as you expect, go into your brokerage account and "modify" your limit order so that it more closely mirrors the most recent bid price.

Remember that ideally you want to be selling option contracts in blocks of 4 or 5 at a time. This reduces your fees immensely; thus, making each transaction more profitable for you down the road.

Should You Use Stop Losses for Your Stocks?

And what in God's pajamas is a stop loss? This is a sell order for your stock that typically is set up to limit the downward price movement of your stock in the stock market. This "limit" order will be triggered and sent to the market as a "market" order when your stock price reaches a particular price. Your stock will then be sold or filled at or just below this price.

Whether or not you should use this tactic, depends on what you might gain or lose by using a stop loss order. The two main advantages of using a stop loss order are that:

- You're able to limit your downside losses to a certain dollar value or percentage of your stock holding.
- And if you're unable to monitor your holdings for a period of time such as during a vacation, a stop loss ensures that you can leave your stocks unattended.

The three major disadvantages are that:

- Higher than normal short-term buying and selling of the stock can trigger the unintentional sale of your holding. This often creates a lost opportunity situation should the stock price quickly rebound back up to its previous level.
- This loss mitigation strategy cannot be used if you're trying to stockpile stock as the price goes down. Stockpiling is the systematic purchase of blocks of shares over a period of time when there is a pullback in the stock price or a minor correction. This is a popular strategy among investors who are looking to buy their stock at below the fair market value, which theoretically creates a margin of safety in the acquisition.

- Unfortunately, your online broker won't allow you to use stop loss orders on your stock positions at the same time as selling covered calls on the stock. This scenario would put your "covered" call into a "naked" position should the underlying security be sold. There would no longer be any collateral (i.e. stock) that covers your call position. From your broker's perspective, this is an extremely risky option position to be in.

Stop loss orders can be a great investment tool to use. However, not every investment situation warrants using this tool to minimize capital loss.

You first need to assess two factors that'll guide you in your decision-making process as to whether or not stop losses are appropriate for your situation:

- First, how do you plan on using this particular holding? Will it be for monthly covered call income? Long-term stock appreciation? Or another strategy altogether?
- Second, what is your exit strategy for this particular investment? At what point do you take money off the table, so to speak?

When you determine how long you'll be holding onto a position along with an appropriate exit strategy, you're in better control of the possible outcomes. Having an exit strategy planned ahead of time allows you to use reason not emotions in arriving at your decision to pull the plug.

As part of your exit strategy decision-making process you should examine the various times when you could conceivably sell your stock positions.

7 Times to Sell Your Stock:

I've boiled down those times when you should cash out of your stock positions to a handful of scenarios. Consider these top seven reasons as being an appropriate time you might want to close out a position:

(1) You've had exceptional stock growth.

When your stock has done well and appreciated above your target price, consider cashing in your position. For example, should you have realized a 50% growth in the appreciation of your stock price, you may wish to turn those paper gains into realized gains by selling your holdings. Exceptional stock growth is an appropriate time to take some money off of the table and look for the next winning investment.

(2) You're seeing poor business performance.

When the company's fundamentals have changed for the worse and the stock price is starting to drop, cut your losses quickly and reposition your capital. Don't hang onto dead money. It's time to get out and move into something that has a higher probability of generating better returns.

A stock that's not keeping up with the rest of the market over time could lag behind for years before a turnaround occurs. Look for a better opportunity with solid fundamentals and upside momentum due to Mr. Market's stamp of approval.

Also, when you've reached your risk tolerance level for loss and a specific holding is keeping you up at night, it's time to liquidate your position. Peace of mind makes sense, right?

(3) You've reached your investment goal.

For some of you investing in the stock market is a means to an end. You've decided to use this particular investment vehicle as a means to generate enough capital so that you could fund another worthwhile, major project. For example, it would be appropriate to move your capital to fund the purchase of a home, to fund a college education or to build a business.

(4) A lucrative opportunity presents itself.

Lucrative investment opportunities do not come around every day. At times, you may need the capital in your stock investment portfolio for another investment opportunity such as an angel capital investment, real estate venture, or the startup of a systematized business. Remember to keep focusing on increasing the speed of your money from one great opportunity to a better one. It also helps to keep an open mind to any and all future possibilities that get you closer to realizing your dreams that much faster.

(5) You've reached a point of being able to retire.

They say that old age is not for wimps. Being almost as old as God, I tend to concur. When you've crunched the numbers and find yourself in the enviable position to retire, you might consider cashing in some of your holdings. The funds could be shifted into other assets during retirement or used to periodically fund part of your retirement. Hopefully, you're able to tap into the tax-free benefits of capital having been generated in a Roth IRA. Now, that would be a smooth move, Ex-Lax.

(6) Your stock portfolio is out of whack.

Being too heavily weighted in one industry or business sector increases your overall portfolio risk or exposure. When your stock investment portfolio gets out of balance, a prudent move would be to sell certain positions and re-investing the proceeds in an unrelated sector or industry. This effectively reduces your overall portfolio risk so that you can preserve your hard-earned capital. More on this in the last chapter.

(7) You experience an unexpected critical expense.

Should you have an unexpected medical bill or related emergency, liquidating some of your stock holdings may be necessary. In this scenario, you may not have a choice. If you've exhausted other options and this one pans out to be your last one, then it may be the only appropriate solution. Not an ideal situation to be faced with, but nevertheless the best one given the circumstances should it arise.

What ultimately governs your decision-making process is your primary objective that of generating cash flow from better and better investment opportunities. Armed with these seven reasons as to when to sell your stock, you now have a much better idea as to when you could be taking money off the table. Once in your brokerage account, you're free to use the proceeds to fund other projects or deal with some of the scenarios previously described.

Your primary objective should be to generate cash flow from better investment opportunities. Now that you have an idea as to possible scenarios for selling a particular stock holding, let's take a look at various exit strategies for your covered call positions.

How to Close an Option Position:

The opposite of selling an option or opening a contract is closing a position by buying back the contract. Recall that when you sold a covered call on stock that you own, you entered a "sell to open" transaction on your trading platform. Now, should you need to close your open call position, you'll "buy to close" to buy back your position, preferably at a lower price than what you sold the calls for.

Here's the step-by-step process:

- Log into your online brokerage account and go to the option position that you want to close out.
- Ensure that you have enough cash in your account in order to execute the close, as well as cover any transaction fees. Closing an option prior to the stock market close on expiration Friday will cost you some money.
- Take a look at the option chain for your particular option contract.
- Enter a "buy to close" order with your online broker. Select a limit order that is between the "ask" and the "mid-price" for that particular option. Recall that the ask price is the higher price between the bid and ask prices posted on the brokerage site. The entire process is the opposite of what you would expect when you sold your options contracts at the lower bid price.
- Wait for the position to be closed out and funds removed from your brokerage account. If your "buy-to-close" is not executed within a few hours, adjust the bid upwards slightly.

4 Times to Buy-to-Close a Call Position:

There are only four scenarios that you need to monitor as to when you could close an option position. Use the following guidelines as to when you could place a "buy to close" order:

(1) Buy-to-close the option if the stock is in danger.

Anytime the business shows major weakness in the fundamentals causing the stock price to drop, place a "buy to close" order. Your immediate goal is to preserve as much of your hard-earned capital as possible.

This means buying back your calls at any price, selling the stock and immediately moving the cash into another position that is more deserving.

(2) Buy-to-close if you have an 80% gain within the first couple of weeks.

When the value of your option contract that you initially received drops by 80%, close your position by buying back the contracts.

Not only do you capture significant gains from your initial contract, you'll be in the enviable position to take advantage of another options play opportunity. This opportunity could be with another stock or occur in the same stock as it jumps back in price.

Here's a tip. As soon as you initially sell an option contract, set a stop loss order for 20% of the initial value that you sold the contracts for. Unlike using a stop loss order for selling your stock holdings, this strategy allows you to automatically capture an 80% gain within the first 2 weeks of the monthly cycle when the option drops in value.

This is the one time that you could consistently use stop loss orders for your option contracts - but not on for your stock holdings.

(3) Buy-to-close if you have a 90% gain in week 3.

Similar to the scenario of capturing an 80% gain, should your current option premium drop below 10% of the original premium paid, close out your position to benefit from the gain. To compensate for the lack of time that's potentially left in the option contract to initiate another option strategy, adjust your expectation from 80 to 90%. In other words, when your option premium is worth only 10% of your original premium received, buy back the contract.

Should you have created a stop-loss order for your option, go into your brokerage account at the beginning of week 3 and modify your option stop-loss orders to reflect the new 10% limit. Consider keeping the modified stop loss order "good until the close" (GTC) on expiration Friday.

Now on occasion your contract cycle will be 5 weeks long instead of the usual 4 weeks. In this case, consider buying back your contracts in week 4 at the 90% gain level and in week 3 for an 80% gain.

(4) Buy-to-close if you want to hang onto a stock that has appreciated in value above the strike price in week 4.

When your stock has appreciated in price above your previously sold strike price and you would like to hang onto it rather than have it called away by expiration Friday, then by all means buy-to-close your option position. By closing your position and simultaneously selling the next month's strike generally at or above the current stock price, you can maintain control over your position.

Which brings us to the subject of the next section. You now know how to close out your option positions under four specific conditions. Let's explore the concept of "rolling" your contracts.

Rolling Positions from One Month to the Next:

Rolling is one of the most common option exit strategies. In simple terms, you close out your current position for the month and immediately sell another position for the next month. This is often done near then end of the current month's option contract.

There are three different rolling strategies you should be aware of:

- Rolling down.
- Rolling out (or forward).
- Rolling out and up.

To best illustrate how each of these rolling strategies works, let me walk you through three hypothetical situations to give you an idea as to how you can use them as part of your arsenal of available timing strategies.

I'll also try to point out not only how to execute each strategy, but also under what conditions to use them.

(1) Rolling down.

When the price of your stock has dropped over the course of the month, rolling down your option contract can offset any losses. You may see signals of the overall market tone being mixed or negative and with the stock's technicals indicating a downward trend in price movement. Using options to protect your stock holdings from catastrophic temporary losses is a common protection strategy.

Rolling down takes advantage of two situations whereby you're buying and selling option contracts:

- You close out your current option position taking a profit on the sale of your current month's option contracts.
- Then you sell the next month's strike price, which is lower than your current month's strike; thus, the term rolling down.

What you're attempting to do is mitigate any potential losses due to the drop in the stock's price. This is accomplished by collecting two option premiums to offset some, if not all, of the decline in the stock price. Any option premiums received reduce your cost basis in your stock and provide you with some downside protection.

The rolling strategy is a far better alternative than hoping and waiting for a rebound in the stock price had you not used any option strategies at all. It's much better than pooping in one hand and wishing in the other to see which one fills up first, wouldn't you concur?

What you'll find reassuring is the ability to still generate income even when your stock has lost value on paper. A typical buy and hold investor would have extensive calluses across their knees from praying so much in the pews. Imagine how high your stress level would be having to wait until your holdings climbed back up out of a hole to get you back to even. It could drive you up the wall.

Time to grab my hand and allow me to walk you step-by-step through a specific example of how the rolling down strategy might play out in the real world. I promise, I'll keep the numbers simple.

In late September, you pick up 100 shares of Wile-E Coyote's ACME stock for $46. Your previous due diligence indicated that the business was fundamentally sound with good growth prospects over the next year and the technical charts showed that ACME was a potential investment play right now.

Upon logging into your brokerage account, you decide to select a slightly in-the-money (ITM) October (45) strike price. You enter a limit order between the bid and mid-price for the option and manage to sell the call for $2 giving you an immediate profit from the cash flow of 4.3% and roughly 2% should the stock get called away. Not a bad start to the month, wouldn't you agree?

Unfortunately, a couple of weeks later, ACME issues a press release announcing that ACME's CEO, Wile-E Coyote, has been seriously injured in a fall. Go figure. This news hammers the stock dropping 15% from $46 to $39. You're stunned. Absolutely flabbergasted.

However, unlike a buy, hold and pray investor, fortunately you've discovered some powerful weapons in this guide. Your focus is now on damage control and mitigating any further losses.

By mid-October, the stock has rebounded from $39 to $42. You decide to "buy to close" the October (45) call for $0.10. Closing your option position produces a net option return of $1.90 per contract, which is the initial $2 call less 10 cents to close the position. Following me so far?

You look at the next month's option chain to see if you can reduce your losses even further. In looking at November's option chain, you decide to roll down to a lower strike and "sell to open" the November (42.50) call for $1.

Notice that the current stock price of $42 is just below the November (42.50) strike price and therefore won't get called away as of the current date.

The total premium received for the month of October is made up of the sale of the October (45) call plus the November (42.50) call less the cost of closing the October (45) call. This amounts to $2.90 per share ($2 + $1 - $0.10) or $290 per contract written.

Your "potential" stock price loss should you not use an option strategy is equal to your initial purchase price of $46 less the current stock price of $42 leaving you with a loss of $4 per share or $400 per 100 shares. This represents a potential loss of approximately 8.7%.

Using your rolling down option strategy, the total premium received reduces your cost basis in the stock, dropping it by $2.90 from $46 to $43.10. Your potential loss in the stock, which is the difference between the new cost basis of $43.10 and the current stock price of $42, is $1.10 per share or $110 for each option contract. This represents only a 2.4% drop versus an 8.7% drop had you not used any options strategies.

If ACME stock closes out the month just above the November (42.50) strike, your loss when the stock is called away (that is sold), has been reduced to $0.60 which is about 1%. This was calculated by comparing the 42.50 strike to the new cost basis in the stock which you reduced to $43.10 from your options plays.

At the end of the day on expiration Friday your broker would deposit $4250 into your brokerage account from the sale of every 100 shares of stock you own. And, your actual loss for each contract for the roughly 2-month period would be $60. That's better than a $400 poke in the eye with a sharp stick.

This first example illustrates that not all options plays will be financially rewarding. However, this particular option strategy can reduce the impact of unforeseen negative circumstances that could potentially have you scrambling. Scrambled eggs are okay, but running around like a chicken with its head cut off is not.

The great news is that just a handful of effective option strategies minimizes the impact of such unanticipated situations. You have tools at your disposal to quickly get back to even despite a major hit to the stock. The important lesson to take away from this particular rolling down option strategy is that it can reduce your potential losses and get you back to even faster.

(2) Rolling out (or forward).

Rolling forward is often used when the stock price has appreciated in value up to the strike price or may even be slightly higher than the strike price. Rolling out makes sense when you would like to hold onto the stock long-term under these two scenarios:

- You want to capture future dividends being generated.
- You see long-term stock price appreciation potential.

Rolling out is a simple 2-step process:

- You close your current position by buying back the contracts.
- You sell the next month's contracts with the same strike price.

Usually, this is either an in-the-money (ITM) or an at-the-money (ATM) call.

More often than not, the current price of the stock will be slightly above your next month's strike. In other words, you will be selling an in-the-money (ITM) call giving you both a good premium and small amount of downside protection.

For this example, we'll be looking at Daffie Duck Enterprises, which you purchased in mid-May for $34.

Daffie Duck Enterprises, symbol DUCK, supplies Accent Inns with their infamous yellow rubber duckies. DUCK rewards its shareholders with a generous annual dividend of almost 4%. The next quarterly dividend will be paid out at the end of June. This is one reason why you would like to hang onto the holding long-term.

Knowing this, you decide to sell an out-of-the-money June (35) call in anticipation that the stock will continue its upward climb on good earnings from the last quarter. The contracts were sold at a little better than the bid price for $0.60 per share.

This transaction generates an immediate cash flow of $60 per contract into your brokerage account, giving you an immediate return of about 1.8%. Granted this is not much in terms of an immediate return. However, should the stock get called away at the June (35) strike, this would generate a total investment return of 4.6%. Unfortunately, you would probably miss out on capturing the dividend being paid out in June.

A couple of weeks later DUCK's stock price has appreciated in value up to the June (35) strike. The current stock price 2 days prior to expiration Friday in June is $34.95 with a very good chance of it being called away. It's time to use the rolling forward exit strategy should you still want to hang onto the stock for its rich dividend.

By waiting for the stock to be called away, you would benefit from a 4.6% return. However, if you felt that the stock still had some upside potential and you wanted to capture the next dividend payment, then rolling forward to the next month makes sense.

The first step is to close out your previous calls by buying back the options at or near the ask price. For this scenario, let's say that you have to pay $1 per share. You've now bought up the value in the stock from your initial price of $34 to the current price of $34.95.

The next step is to immediately sell next month's same strike, thereby rolling forward your position. From the option chain for DUCK, you determine that selling at or near the bid would bring in $1.15 in immediate cash.

Notice that the current stock price of $34.95 is below the July (35) strike price and therefore won't get called away as of the current date.

The total premium received for this time period is made up of the sale of the June (35) call plus the July (35) call less the cost of closing the June (35) call. Quickly doing the math, you have $0.60 + $1.15 - $1. This amounts to $0.75 per share of option's premiums plus $1 of stock price appreciation for a total potential return of 5%.

Given that you're eligible to capture the next dividend of say $0.30 per share this increases your total potential return to 6% and all within roughly a 1-month window.

Recall that the initial goal was to capture the upside growth in the price appreciation of the stock along with a modest option premium. As the month of June played out you were able to see that the company did in fact reach your target expectation. The choice that you'll often be faced with is do I take money off the table right away or let it ride a little longer for another month.

If you did nothing in June and the stock closes <u>above</u> the June (35) strike it will be called away and you'll have cash in your account ready for the next opportunity. The actual total return would be 4.6%. A pretty decent return, wouldn't you agree?

If you did nothing in June and the stock closes <u>below</u> the June (35) strike, you only capture the 1.8% option return. However, you can pop back into the option market with an appropriate call strategy or sell the stock and move into a better opportunity altogether.

The one downside of using a "wait and see" approach and not rolling forward is that your initial call option growth strategy generates a minimal amount of cash. By using a growth strategy, you're hoping that you'll make the majority of your money when the stock price appreciates up to or past the strike.

Using the rolling out strategy generates more upfront cash into your brokerage account as opposed to waiting and seeing.

As you can see by analyzing the cash production potential of various scenarios, you'll be more effective in generating a consistent stream of cash flowing into your brokerage account.

In the next scenario, should your stock continue to rise up past your 35 strike, then you can always use the strategy of rolling out and up.

(3) Rolling out and up.

This strategy is best used when your stock price has appreciated beyond your option strike price and you would like to hang onto the stock in anticipation of further price appreciation.

You're looking for positive growth signals in the stock and market as evidenced by solid fundamentals and technicals for the market and the stock.

Rolling out and up takes advantage of two situations whereby you're buying then selling option contracts:

- You close out your current option position taking a profit on the sale of your current month's option contracts.
- Then you sell the next month's higher strike price. This could be an at-the-money (ATM) strike or more commonly an out-of-the-money (OTM) strike.

The net result of this process is that you end up buying the increased equity value of the stock along with receiving another option premium resulting in an overall return that is higher. Doing nothing, your option would probably have been exercised on expiration Friday and you would have just received the original option premium for your efforts.

Let's assume that you purchased shares from the agricultural giant Elmar Fudd Limited, symbol FUDD, at the end of January at $25 per share. During the course of the day, you also sold at-the-money ATM covered call options with a February (25) strike for $1.00 each.

Your initial strategy was to create a pure income play with the stock and you expected it to be called away at the end of February should it stay above the 25 strike.

This income strategy provides you with a healthy immediate return of 4%, which is just above the upper limit of our monthly sweet spot zone.

Let's assume that by mid-February, FUDD has appreciated 8% in price from $25 to $27. It looks as if the stock will be called away come expiration Friday in one week's time. If you now decide to modify your exit strategy and hold onto the stock capturing some of this price appreciation, then your best bet would be to use a roll out and up strategy.

The first step is to close out your initial February (25) strike by buying back the contracts. In this case they were bought back for

$2, which was the current asking price for the contracts. Buying back the February (25) contracts, buys back the equity in the stock.

The second step is to select a higher strike price for the next month's option contract, preferably just above the current price of the stock. A March (28) out-of-the money call, was selected since the stock was trading at $27. Note that the current stock price is lower than the option strike price; therefore, the stock won't get called away as of the current date. This last transaction netted an option premium of $0.50 per share.

Allow me to summarize what has transpired so far. By using a combination of buying and selling option contracts you've captured the price appreciation in the stock price and set yourself up for some additional upside potential. Woo hoo! That beats trying to nail Jell-O to the basement wall. Wouldn't you agree?

The total premium received for this month is made up of the sale of the February (25) call plus the March (28) call less the cost of closing the February (25) call. Your total premium generated for February is going to be a slight loss ($1.00 + $0.50 - $2.00 = -$0.50).

This amounts to a loss of $0.50 per share, which is what you would have paid out of your brokerage account to buy back the value in the stock. However, you've benefited from the stock price appreciation which has gone from $25 to $27. This represents a 6% net increase after factoring in the cost of buying back the equity. The maximum upside potential for this combination of strategies should the stock close above the March (28) strike is 10%. Not a bad return over the course of several weeks, if I do say so myself.

The rolling forward and up strategy takes advantage of the price appreciation potential of the stock. This particular strategy is an important one to employ under two scenarios:

- You would like to hang onto the stock for the dividends it's paying out.
- You would like to capture the upside appreciation in the stock price.

A case in point is that by taking an active role in your investing you're better able to take advantage of opportunities as they unfold. You might enter the stock market using one cash generation strategy only to discover a more lucrative position could be created.

Smart investors are always looking for potentially better opportunities from which to profit. You've been empowered to do the same. You now have an idea as to how to make those judgment calls as to whether it's more advantageous to switch to a different exit strategy or stay the course with your initial decision.

In the above example, should your FUDD stock and the market as a whole show technical signs of leveling out, then switching from your growth strategy to a pure income play for the next option contract month of April may be the way to go. Should FUDD begin trading sideways, selling ATM calls for the immediate income optimizes your option income.

And should FUDD continue its upward climb using a growth strategy in April is a good option. You not only continue to capture the immediate premium, but you also have some stock price appreciation potential built in.

You may be saying to yourself: May I be excused? My brain is quite full now. Let me close by summarizing what we've covered so far.

Summary of the 6 Option Exit Strategies:

Here's a summary of the 6 option exit strategies discussed in this guide and when it's appropriate to employ the various exit strategies discussed.

(1) Take no action during the month.

If no advantage may be gained by using a particular exit strategy and there have been no changes in the fundamentals or technicals of a stock, then take no alternate course of action.

(2) Close your option position.

Use a "buy-to-close" exit strategy to lock in your profits. Then patiently wait for another option play on the same stock to occur in the same month. You should buy back your contracts in the first 2 weeks when you have a gain of 80%. And buy back your contracts during the 3rd week if you see a 90% gain.

(3) Close your option position and sell your stock.

When your stock is no longer fundamentally sound or the stock market is in danger, it may be prudent to move your capital into cash until the dust and excitement subside.

(4) Roll down your position.

Should your stock temporarily decline in price and you still want to keep it, possibly for a dividend payout, then look at rolling down your position to offer some downside protection and mitigate any potential losses.

(5) Roll out your position.

This scenario may play out when your stock price is now greater than your initial purchase price as you approach expiration Friday and you would like to keep the holding. It can be an effective strategy when you want to capture a quarterly dividend payment. Rolling out should be done if you have a neutral outlook for the stock and the market.

(6) Roll out and up.

This strategy works best when you have a bullish outlook for the stock and the market. When your stock price is greater than your initial purchase price as you approach expiration Friday and you would like to keep the holding, look into rolling up and forward.

In summary, your overall investment objective is to use exit strategies to make money and to minimize potential losses. The two go hand in hand. Preserving your capital investment should be your top priority. As Phil Town in Rule 1 says:

"Rule #1 is to never lose money."

Being actively engaged as an investor allows you to take advantage of certain opportunities that increase your probability of generating superior returns in the stock market.

Timing Guidelines for Moving into the Market:

A common challenge that beginning investors are faced with is in determining which investment strategy provides the optimal return for a given situation. For example, what strategy should you focus on when the markets are flat?

Use this simple guideline to help with the decision-making process. It'll provide you with a starting point from which to base your decisions as to which strategy may be the most appropriate.

When using these guidelines, also consider incorporating these three factors into your decision matrix:

1. Your comfort level for risk,
2. Your current skill set, and
3. The time you realistically have available for your investing.

You have a couple of choices to make. I like to use both the S&P 500 as well as the stock in determining which strategy I'm going to use. If you decide to use the monthly appreciation for the S&P 500, then look at the SPY ETF for your growth analysis.

Should you prefer looking at your specific stock holdings, then check out the monthly growth rate of the stock's price. Here are some numbers to crunch:

- If the overall market and your stock have appreciated greater than 3%, hold onto your stock and rub your hands together like a giddy child in a candy store. No need to sell calls as the stock may continue appreciating in value faster than a safe option return for your holding.
- When your stock or the market are growing at a monthly rate of 1% to 3%, consider selling out-of-the-money OTM calls. Your focus should be on growth when you're in this enviable position.
- When your stock or the market are flat, meaning that the growth rate is ± 1%, consider selling at-the-money ATM calls or slightly in-the-money ITM calls. Your focus should be on income production, especially if the markets are going nowhere.
- When your stock or the market are trending lower and you're seeing a negative monthly growth rate of -1 to -3%, consider selling in-the-money ITM calls that focus on protection.
- When your stock or the market have a negative monthly growth rate in excess of 3%, consider moving to cash &/or buy an undervalued dividend stock.

These detailed timing insights should provide you with an additional boost of confidence. Now, you're in the enviable position of knowing enough about buying market leaders and selling covered calls on those holdings.

Imagine benefitting from a monthly stream of income that could fund a family vacation, reduce your current debt load, or allow you to move into your dream home. Wouldn't that be skookum?

≈

7

STRUCTURING YOUR STOCK INVESTMENT PORTFOLIO

So far, this guide has shown you how to identify stocks with upside growth potential and how to create an additional stream of income from selling covered calls. You've discovered a number of timing strategies for both your stock holdings and option positions, thus enabling you to move safely into and out of the markets.

In this final chapter we're going to help you structure your stock portfolio so that you reduce your level of risk and exposure in the markets. As well, I'll share a couple of routines designed to help you monitor your positions so that you're not caught off guard by any significant changes in the marketplace.

Creating a Diversified Stock Portfolio:

What in the Wide Wide World of Sports does diversification mean? Depending on who you talk it can become an entirely different animal altogether. Ask a mutual fund adviser and they'll tout that diversification is best achieved by buying an index or basket of 100 or more stocks through some type of fund. On the flip side are the various investment gurus who suggest holding just a handful of personally selected stocks.

So, how do you create a diverse portfolio of investments? One that'll provide upside potential and downside protection of your capital?

Since you'll be hand-selecting the vast majority of your stocks, here are seven key factors to integrate into your investment portfolio in order to create an appropriate level of diversification:

(1) Diversify across Asset Classes.

You've embarked on a journey to become a lifelong investor. Ideally, your overall investment portfolio should contain not only stocks, but also investments from other asset classes.

And what do I mean by other asset classes? Real estate rental property, systematized businesses, fixed-income investments like bonds, and even commodities like oil and gold, allow you spread out your risk across various investment markets. Should one market be trending lower another unrelated one may be heading higher.

By investing in various asset classes over time, you create a better balance in preserving and growing your overall capital. Ultimately, this should be one of your long-term investment objectives. The vast majority of self-made millionaires use a multi-faceted approach to wealth creation. And so should you. Makes sense, right?

(2) Diversify within the Stock Market.

Your stock portfolio should contain holdings from various groups of stocks that are classified by size and characteristics. For example, a core amount of your investment capital could be invested in large cap stocks, with a smaller percentage being spread across small or mid cap stocks. Incidentally, the term "large cap" refers to large capitalization. In other words, this is a corporation that has accumulated a large amount of capital.

In a booming economy, you may find that holdings in the small-cap universe prove to be the winners. During an economic slowdown, dividend-paying stocks may out-perform the small or mid-cap stock universes. When you diversify your capital within the stock market, you can often benefit from the changing tides that occur every 5 to 6 years.

(3) Diversify across 11 Economic Sectors.

Companies traded in the stock market can be grouped based on the nature or purpose of the business. We currently categorize all businesses by assigning them to one of 11 economic sectors, such as technology, energy and health care.

A popular rule of thumb is to allocate no more than 20% of your investment capital in any one economic sector. Doing so provides you with a better-balanced portfolio. Should one economic sector go out of favour with the market, another can often take its place. When you spread out your capital, you improve your odds of overall portfolio growth.

(4) Diversify across the Globe.

You may have come across the expression: God created the world, everything else is made in China. The United States has undeniably the most vibrant stock markets in the world. However, don't discount the growth potential in emerging foreign markets that may be growing faster than the U.S. economy. At a minimum, you should actively seek out companies that have a global exposure. This can be done with U.S. based companies that export more than 30% of their goods or services overseas. Also check out ADR's, which are foreign companies that trade on U.S. exchanges. The tag ADR stands for American Depository Receipt.

For our neighbours to the north, consider exposing yourself to Canadian companies in the financial sector or base materials. Canada has one of the strongest financial systems in the world and is a commodity-based economy.

Another collection of countries to investigate are the BRICS countries. Brazil, Russia, India, China and South Africa have growing middle classes that are becoming more apt to purchase products from international players. Start, by focusing your attention on U.S. and Canadian companies with international exposure, as well as those foreign businesses listed as ADRs on the U.S. stock exchanges.

(5) Diversify across Time.

Investing should be done on a regular basis in order to tap into opportunities as they present themselves. When you have cash sitting on the sidelines, you're able to take advantage of miss pricings in the market. This often allows you to buy into positions with a margin of safety.

(6) Diversify across Investment Accounts.

As you know, not all investment accounts are created equal. Some accounts allow you to grow your investments tax-free. Others defer the tax you pay until a future date. The smart investor will diversify their holdings across these types of accounts based on the specific advantages and limitations of each.

You're probably familiar with the 401(k) [RRSP in Canada], which creates a tax deduction up front in return for taxable income once money is being withdrawn during retirement. Some employers will match your retirement contributions up to an allowable maximum. Should you be in this generous position, it makes sense to take advantage of the match up to the allowable maximum set up by your employer.

The Roth IRA [TFSA in Canada] is a tax-free account. Any investment capital deposited has already been taxed and can grow and compound over time to be used tax free at a future date. Also, self-directed IRA accounts usually have many more investment choices beyond just a small selection of mutual funds, ETF's or bonds typically offered in 401(k) accounts.

(7) *Diversify across Investment Strategies.*

It should come as no surprise that some investment strategies work better under certain economic conditions than others. Consistently using a few time-tested solid performers will help to boost your overall returns. Sticking with a proven system over time better prepares you for changing market conditions.

Hopefully, you have a better idea as to how you could structure your investment portfolio to not only take advantage of opportunities as they present themselves, but more importantly to preserve your hard-earned capital.

Let's take a look at a couple of routines to follow that'll help you monitor your progress and keep you out of deep do do.

(1) Daily Routine:

Under ideal circumstances, you'll want to check on your holdings twice a day, 10 minutes in the morning and 10 minutes at the end of the day. This will keep you abreast of what is happening in the markets and enable you to quickly react to any major developments and keep you out of any serious trouble. Let me describe how your day might unfold under these ideal circumstances.

I know for myself, sometimes I wake up grumpy, other times I let her sleep. First things first, after you've had your green drink smoothie or cup of java in the morning, log into your online brokerage account, so that you can check out how the overall markets and your open positions are doing. Here's a 6-step routine to consider following:

Step #1: Check out the overall market sentiment and any global news that may directly affect your current holdings.

Step #2: Check for any recent news posts for each stock that you're holding. This can be easily accomplished by clicking on the news tab associated with each stock. If the news is positive, think about how you could capture any gains now or down the road. Should the news be negative, consider an appropriate exit strategy based on what you've picked up in this guide. Also check each stock's technical chart to verify if there were any gaps overnight that could affect your current exit strategy planned for each holding.

Step #3: Take any appropriate action if need be later that day. Do you need to close a position? Do you need to re-allocate capital? Be proactive in your approach. By checking on and making any adjustment to your positions first thing in the morning, you free your mind from worry. Having a clear stress-free mind makes the balance of the day easier to stomach.

Step #4: If you're able to do so at the end of the trading day around 3:30 PM EST, review the news to see if there is anything negative that might affect your positions. If you're unable to do so right before the markets close, try to verify how your holdings are doing later that evening.

Step #5: Take a quick look at a technical chart for each stock to make sure that they're behaving according to your trading plan. Minor fluctuations are the norm. Expect to see a gentle wave-like pattern. However, a free-fall descent of a stock's price is not.

Step #6: Take any appropriate action if need be. Depending on what the situation is, you may wish to wait a day or so to see if it resolves itself.

There you have it in a nutshell, a simple daily routine designed to give you peace of mind and react proactively to major developments. You won't be feeling as nervous as a small nun at a penguin shoot by doing so. Moving on to your quarterly review. Are you ready, Freddy?

(2) Quarterly Review:

Unfortunately, the way most brokerage houses report on your portfolio progress isn't helpful to you. Your online discount broker is probably posting the daily change in your portfolio like mine does.

Remember, constipated people, don't give a crap. I ignore this data since I'm not a day trader trying to make a buck on a daily basis. I'm not too concerned about monitoring the day-to-day changes that occur. What I'm more interested in is the monthly flow of cash that occurs when selling covered calls or received from dividends. And to get a better sense of how my overall portfolio is doing, I focus my attention on my quarterly progress.

There are two major metrics I like to monitor. The first is how much cash I've been able to generate during the quarter from my options plays. In other words, what is the net return on my options. Not only do I like to know if my overall portfolio is generating an average monthly return of 2 to 3%, I'm also interested in the dollar value that's associated with this return.

The second metric I track is my portfolio growth. Has my overall portfolio appreciated in value over the quarter or lost some ground?

The stock market can move up and down like an ocean wave over the course of a month. When you embrace this notion that the stock market doesn't move to new heights in a linear fashion, it becomes easier to accept the constant corrections occurring. This is why checking your portfolio performance on a quarterly basis makes more sense than a daily or weekly assessment.

Tracking my growth rate from options plays gives me a psychological boost. It should build your confidence level as well.

Tracking my quarterly income from my option premiums received allows me to better plan my future withdrawals. Both metrics tracked on a quarterly basis empower me to make better asset allocation decisions.

As a side note, even though you may have a stock holding that has lost some "book" value over the course of the month, it's not until you sell those shares that you actually realize a loss. Better yet, when you control a number of options contracts, you can still generate a positive flow of cash into your brokerage account.

This notion should encourage you because it illustrates that you can make money in the stock market despite the market going through a short correction period. Covered calls do provide you with greater income generation possibilities. Wouldn't you feel more confident if this scenario played out for your portfolio?

~

CONCLUSION

This guide focused on how to select market leaders in the stock market to generate a monthly income stream from covered calls being sold on those holdings.

You started your journey into discovering more about the wonderful world of stock investing by initially exploring what options were. Three main benefits to using covered calls were outlined as far as being able to tap into a monthly stream of income, reduce your risk and accelerate your wealth creation.

Chapter two had you exploring how to set yourself up for success as a covered call writer. You looked at the three smart investment vehicles self-made millionaires use that of becoming financially intelligent, acquiring assets and building systematized businesses. intelligent, acquiring assets and building systematized businesses.

We discussed how to increase the speed of your money and what it meant to reach a point of critical mass with your investments.

Chapter three delved into how to create a watchlist of heavy hitters, those businesses that are potential market leaders. Taking a top down view of the markets, you were also provided with seven global trends to keep your eye on that could provide you with some potential stock investing opportunities. Along with this, you learned about ten super sources of information to help you find potential stocks.

Chapter four was all about assessing the profitability of those stocks on your watchlist. You were exposed to nine simple assessment criteria for identifying market leaders. And you learned about seven common types of economic moats that can create a competitive advantage for a particular business. This was followed up by a means of quickly assessing if the management team has the shareholders' interests at heart.

In Chapter five you discovered how to use just three effective covered call strategies to generate a monthly stream of income and protect your holdings. You now know when and how to use the growth, income and protection strategies along with a number of specific tips designed to help you generate consistent returns.

Chapter six dealt with how to best enter and exit positions; whether that be a stock holding or covered call. A number of timing tips were discussed from when to enter a stock position to exiting your covered calls. Several scenarios were discussed in detail so that you could move into and out of positions safely.

Finally, in Chapter seven you touched on how to best structure your investment portfolio. You also discovered a simple way of monitoring your positions thus giving you some peace of mind in knowing how to proactively handle any situations.

Should you like some additional insights into stock investing, I encourage you to pick up a copy of the special report "Investing in Momentum Stocks Secrets". You'll receive some great insights along with some additional tools.

In closing, let me share some sage advice passed on by my dad with you:

If you have a dream, protect it. Don't let someone else tell you that you can't do it. And don't let someone else's opinion of what you can and cannot do dictate your life's journey.

You've embarked on an incredible journey of exploring the wonderful world of stock investing. Time to predict your future and prepare for it.

To you ongoing success as an investor.

~

Printed in Great Britain
by Amazon

33275649R00071